ASYMMETRICAL 2

Philosophical Investigations into Thinking, Reflection, Action and Agency

JONATHAN CHAPMAN

UK Book Publishing.com

ASYMMETRICAL 2

Philosophical Investigations into Thinking, Reflection, Action and Agency

Design, typesetting and publishing by UK Book Publishing

www.ukbookpublishing.com

ISBN: 978-1-916572-42-3

It all starts with the Pythagoreans. The argument took the shape "Do you ask what it is made of – earth, fire, water, etc?" Or do you ask, "What is its *pattern*?"

Gregory Bateson: Form, Substance & Difference

It is perfectly true, as the philosophers say, that life must be understood backwards. But they forget the other proposition, that it must be lived forwards.

Søren Kierkegaard, Journals

TABLE OF CONTENTS

I. INTRODUCTION

1. Hanging together

The cultural revival of Europe in the 12th century was grounded in a largely unified conception that the way the world worked was apparent in its observable structure. This model was for the most part based on interpretations of the works of Aristotle. The central idea was the idea of a substance, an individuated entity whose substantial form governed the way in which it evolved. In this model, cognition wasn't seen to present any particular problems, because a human being was understood as a substance whose substantial form included the capacity for rational intelligence.

This model, now called hylomorphism, became untenable in the course of the Scientific Revolution of the 17th century, during which the ontology of substantial form was replaced by a mechanical model in which the underlying evolution of a physical system came to be described in terms of mechanical devices: balances, levers, pulleys, spindles, and screws.

The mechanical model itself has long been superseded as the scientific image of the world, but the problem it created – the separation between apparent form and underlying dynamics, between the observable and the real – has remained.

Why is this? Aristotelian thinking was a synthesis, in which the idea of substantial form brought a unity of explanation not only to physical systems, but also the principles of living beings and the foundations of conceptual thinking. This explains why modern science doesn't have the same scope. One requirement of any plausible ontology (that is, any global inventory of entities and events) is that it must include itself within that inventory. However, as Erwin Schrödinger noted in his essay *Mind and Matter*, in order to create an objective discipline, the scientist's opening gambit is to exclude the subject of cognizance, and by extension, conceptual structure, from the target domain of science. Science doesn't investigate itself, and thereby investigates a world of which it itself is not a part. Science is, inescapably, incomplete.

As things stand, therefore, we have reached an impasse. We have a scientific understanding of nature articulated, at the most fundamental level, as a set of mathematical models in physics. At the same time, those mathematical models have nothing to say about the familiar world of our own experience of existence, and its explanations, justifications, interests and values. We have at least two different images of the world and no obvious means of integrating them.

The central problem posed by the scientific revolution is the relationship between the physical and the conceptual. By physical I don't mean material; the ontology of modern physics doesn't have a concept of materiality in the way that it has concepts of fields, forces, energy, mass and charge. Similarly, by conceptual I don't mean mental. A mental event, such as someone engaged in solving a mathematical puzzle or thinking through an ethical dilemma, is still a physical event. What is conceptual is the meaning of the event, not the modality of its instantiation.

Conceptual models apply to domains of application through analogy. This is possible because model and target are organised into analogous patterns. This is relatively apparent in the mathematical sciences, but is obscured elsewhere by the forms of natural language, particularly the way the propositions of language are structured as subjects and predicates.

In its simplest form, my proposal in this essay is that, firstly, meaningful concepts can be co-located with physical events because they can be shaped into analogous patterns, and, secondly, that these analogous patterns can be discerned by beings with the detachment from the flow of events that comes from self-aware rationality.

The argument is governed by two very simple but very abstract ontological propositions. Firstly, the characteristic feature of the human condition is its interiority. This inwardness has multiple aspects. There is the interiority that is a corollary of the fact that the inner life is hidden behind the surface of outward appearance, so that our own inner life is private and the inner lives of others can only be inferred from their outer expression. There is the diachronic interiority that is a corollary of the temporal sequencing and path-dependent structuring of events in a life: there is a single continuity to these events, and we can't pause, jump, switch, split from or merge lives. There is also cultural interiority; we exist at a particular place and time and at a specific level of civilisational evolution and cultural and technological acquisition.

Secondly, conceptual structures can't exist independently, they are not products of nature. Conceptual structures cannot actualise themselves; in order to be actualised, they have to be instantiated by an actualised entity such as a human being.

The idea is that these two ontologies are connected. The evolution of natural entities can be shaped by conceptual patterns because thinking is the actualisation of conceptual structures by human minds. This actualisation is dependent on self-awareness and the capacity for reflection and introspection that is the characteristic feature of the human condition. In the actualisation of conceptual structures, the human mind acquires an analogous structure and with it the pattern of rationality. Reflective rationality is the outcome of the co-location and interaction of the patterning that flows from interiority with the patterning that flows from conceptualisation.

The spirit of this enquiry is that things don't happen at random, but equally, we shouldn't impose on events more necessity than is necessary. The American philosopher Wilfred Sellars suggested, in his essay *Philosophy and the Scientific Image of Man*, that philosophical reflection was ultimately motivated by the desire to understand *how things in the broadest possible sense...hang together*. This seems to me a sensible goal to aim for. It allows for an ontological and explanatory pluralism, avoiding the tendency to assume there is ultimately a single pattern, or single operative principle, which we might be able to understand by synthesising our knowledge into a single conceptual structure. At the same time, it recognises that there is just a single cosmos, and, at minimum, everything is connected, if only through loose associations of mutual accommodation, adjustment and adaptation.

The essay is organised into three related parts. The first is concerned with metaphysical thinking as it has evolved in Europe, and more lately in the wider world, over the last 900 years, under the pressure of scientific and technological development. It is intended to provide background and context.

The second part is concerned with conceptual structure. Conceptual structures are like engineering structures: they are constructions of the human mind but, at the same time, constrained by the principles of conceptual construction. Just as bridges and towers must be built within engineering constraints, conceptual models and conceptual objects must be built within rational constraints.

The third part is then concerned with the relationship between human existence and conceptual actualisation. It seeks to answer the question: On what basis is it possible for human minds to actualise concepts and think conceptually? The argument here is that only minds capable of reflective self-awareness can support the self-referencing that is necessary to conceptual thinking.

II. A BRIEF HISTORY OF ONTOLOGICAL THINKING

2. The Aristotelian synthesis

Two connected developments marked the beginning, in the 12th century, of the intellectual revival of Europe. One was the establishment of the first universities and the development of the scholastic method of instruction. This was an approach to learning from authoritative sources through commentary, interpretation and disputation. The other was the increase in contact between Europe and the Islamic world through channels in the Levant, in Sicily and in Spain, which led to the translation from Arabic into Latin of the contemporary knowledge of the Islamic world, including its inheritance from ancient Greece.

These translations included the cosmology of Ptolemy, the geometry of Euclid, the algebra of Al-Khwarizmi, some of the works of Archimedes and most of the works of Aristotle. In the 13th century, better translations of Aristotle, directly from the original Greek, were made by William of Moerbeke. These were used, most notably by Thomas Aquinas, as the basis for the synthesis of Aristotelian natural philosophy and Christian theology that would be taught in the new universities and which they would still be teaching in the middle of the 17th century.

This synthesis provided the ontological and logical armature of the European world-view prior to the Scientific Revolution. In this section I sketch the basic structure of Aristotelian thinking, to show why the new sciences would cause a crisis for the model and inevitably lead to a revolution in that world-view.

What were the main features of the Aristotelian ontology? Arguably the four most significant works of Aristotle from this perspective are the *Categories*, which is concerned with what can be said; the *Physics*, which deals with the organising principles of nature; *De Anima*, which is concerned with the organising principles of living things; and the *Metaphysics*, which is concerned with first principles in epistemology, logic and, in the discussion of the nature of substance, ontology.

A good place to start is with the *Categories*. The term category comes from the Greek *katêgoriai,* meaning that which can be predicated of something, that is, that which can be said about it. Aristotle identified ten such categories of what can be said about something: in the first place, there is its substance, that is, what it is, and then there are its properties. These properties can in turn be divided into nine categories. Seven of these categories are static: quality, quantity, relationships, location in space, location in time, conformation, and attributes. The other two are dynamic: what the entity is doing and what is being done to it. The link between what something is and what can be said about it rests on the fact that the ontological relationship between substances and properties has the same form as the logical relationship between subject and predicate.

The main distinction between the categories is that substances exist independently while every other category of being exists dependently. What is predicated in the other categories depends on the existence of a substance. We must say, at least implicitly, *This something is x* and only then can we say *X is here now*, or *X is lying over there*, or *X is suffering badly*.

This doesn't mean that the subject of predication must be a substance. We can also say *Red is a colour* or *Seven is a number* or *Suffering is wrong*, where the subject of predication is not a substance, but the subject of predication in these cases doesn't have an independent existence; it too must be a property of a substance.

A predicate such as *plant* that can be applied to many individual subjects is a universal term, while one that can be applied to only one individual thing is a particular term. The structure in each category of predicate, including that of substance, is a hierarchy. At the highest level is the genus; the genus is differentiated into species; and the species are differentiated into individuals. So, for example, we can say of something that *X is a plant*, *X is an oak* or *X is the solitary oak by the lake*. In each case, *x* is an individual *this something*.

A universal term such as *plant* is one that can be said of many things, while a particular term such as *the solitary oak by the lake* can be said of only one thing. This is why universal terms can be predicated of categories other than substances. Certain terms can only be applied to individuals, so they can only apply to substances, because only a substance can be an individual entity.

The *Categories* is thought to be an early work and the analysis doesn't contain any direct reference to a theory of change. Change requires composition; for anything to change, at least one component of that thing must remain the same and at least one must become different. Something that isn't composite cannot change, it can only continue unchanged or cease to exist. In the *Physics*, Aristotle identifies the basis of change as the composite of form and matter. This is the basic premise of hylomorphism. Change is a function of the composition of matter and form, and the subject matter of the *Physics* is everything that evolves through the composition of matter and form – which ultimately refers to everything in nature.

In this framework, form and matter are relational terms. For example, with regard to a roll of cloth, the cloth is the form and the thread from which it is woven is the matter. However, with regard to a garment such as a cloak that could be cut from the cloth, the cloak is now the form and the cloth is now the matter.

In order to avoid an infinite regress, everything was thought to be composed ultimately of different proportions of the four basic elements of earth, water, air and fire, and these were conceived of as four different forms of an otherwise characterless prime matter.

It's important to remember that matter in this framework is not static. In modern thinking, we see the thread, the cloth and the garment as three configurations of the same underlying matter, which we would probably describe in terms of its chemical substance or molecular structure. In this schema, the matter cannot be eliminated, only reconfigured, and this is why we think in terms of materialism.

This is not the case with the Aristotelian schema. When there is change, it is the matter that is being modified by the form. Matter becomes the fundamental subject of change and form is the source of that change. This is how the entry on Aristotle's metaphysics in the *Stanford Encyclopedia of Philosophy* describes the idea:

> Whether we are thinking of natural objects, such as plants and animals, or artifacts, such as houses, the requirements for generation are the same. We do not produce the matter (to suppose that we do leads to an infinite regress) nor do we produce the form (what could we make it out of?); rather, we put the form into the matter, and produce the compound. Both the matter and the form must pre-exist. But the source of motion in both cases – what Aristotle calls the "moving cause" of the coming to be – is the form.

Providing an explanation of an entity or event means identifying its causes. Cause in this context means *explanation* or *account* rather than *antecedent state* or *underlying driver*. There were four components to an explanation of how things come about: the material cause, the formal cause, the efficient cause, and the final cause. To provide a sufficient explanation of change therefore meant providing the complete set of four causes.

The material cause is the matter, such as the cloth in my example. The formal cause is the form or shape that is put into or given to the cloth – the cloak, in this example. The efficient cause is the artisan who makes the cloak from the cloth, and the final cause is the purpose for which the cloak is made; let's say to protect the wearer from the weather. Both form and matter already exist, so change is a process in which some form is put into some matter, initiated by some agent, for the sake of some purpose.

How does this theory of change impact the understanding of substances? In the framework of hylomorphism, it is the form that makes something a *this something*, so it is this that becomes the substantial form of an entity, and it is therefore substantial form that becomes the primary cause of something's being what it is. If we want to explain why there exists a *this something*, a hylomorphic analysis would say that some substantial form is present in the material components of the body.

It should be said that this is not always clear in Aristotle. It may seem to follow that, because primary substances are individuals, they should be described by particular terms; while attributes, species and genera should be described by universal terms. However, Aristotle made contradictory statements, often linking substantial form to a universal term rather than a particular term, and this remains a crux when it comes to interpretation. This is from same article in the *Stanford Encyclopedia of Philosophy*:

> The idea that substantial forms are particulars is supported by Aristotle's claims that a substance is "separable and this something" (chôriston kai tode ti), that there are no universals apart

from their particulars, and that universals are not substances. On the other side, the idea that substantial forms are universals is supported by Aristotle's claims that substances are, par excellence, the definable entities, that definition is of the universal, and that it is impossible to define particulars.

Hylomorphism is a version of essentialism, and this raises one of the fundamental difficulties for any kind of essentialism. It's again useful to keep in mind the difference between this way of thinking and modern assumptions. In modern usage, definitions are attached to words and concepts, and we think of the definition capturing their meaning. In classical Greek thinking, definitions applied to the objects rather than to the terms and concepts used to describe them. When it came to translating the idea of a definition into Latin, the translators came up with the term *essence* to describe the what it is to be something, and this is where the term *essentialism* comes from. Essentialism is the idea that things have definitions; its contraries are *nominalism,* the idea that it is terms that have definition, and *conceptualism,* the idea that it is concepts that have definition.

The problem that all forms of essentialism face is that many things can be said of the same object: it is a tree, an oak, and the solitary oak by the lake. Which of these is the substantial form? The terms *tree* and *oak* are universals, they can be said of many things, so that doesn't explain what makes an object *this something.* The particular term *the solitary oak by the lake,* on the other hand, can only be said of one thing. That would suggest that the substantial form is what is described in particular terms, because only a particular term can describe an individual entity.

However, that would create a problem, because it would make *the solitary oak by the lake* into the definition of the entity, and this would be at odds with the idea that substantial form has definition and what has definition is identified by universal terms. What role is being played by species and the genera, if the individual already has sufficient definition in particular terms?

Why would it be a problem? The reason is that a thing is already what it is now and the particular term captures that completeness. But definitions are meant to explain not just what something is now but what it is going to be, its teleology. In hylomorphism, change in something is analysed in terms of movement towards the completion of its definition, and if everything is already completely what it is, there would be no change. We tend to think in terms of change as the evolution of something being driven forward, whereas in this model it is better to think of change as something being drawn towards its completed state.

To understand this, we need to understand the conception of change as a change of state from potential to actual and the coupling of this analysis to the idea of a definition as the essence of something. In the development of Aristotle's thinking, form seems to have meant originally something like the shape given to a material, and then later acquired the sense of activity and actualisation of potentiality.

Potentiality is a capacity, in the sense that a length of thread is potentially a roll of cloth and a roll of cloth is potentially a cloak. To Aristotle, actuality has priority over potentiality and this is the case in giving an account; the account must start with what is actualised, not with what is only potential.

Hylomorphism and the theory of the four causes do not provide by themselves an account of what is motivating the structure. The efficient and final causes are the proximate cause of the form being applied to the matter, but the form and the matter exist beforehand, and the efficient cause and the final cause are not free agents, so to speak, but themselves instruments of a larger design.

This larger design is organised around the idea of change as the evolution from what is potential to what is actual and the connection of this dynamic to the concept of completion. What is being actualised is the substantial form, conceptualised as the definition or essence of a thing. This in turn means that that evolution must be towards completion or finitude. An entity is potentially some substantial form, and the process of change is the actualisation of that substantial form. Change is conceived of as teleological, in the sense that what motivates the actualisation of potentiality is a change from a less to a more complete state. Because completion is conceptualised in terms of the definition or essence, potentiality means in this context the capacity to evolve into the more complete state in which the definition is actualised.

Actuality has priority in substances because things evolve towards an end, or *telos,* as the acorn evolves into the oak tree, and that actualisation of form is the direction taken by all natural processes. The progression of forms, from thread, to cloth, to garment, is a progression of both form and material, with the form of one stage becoming the matter of the next. In this framework, the completion of the process is reached when the form becomes the definition and can evolve no further. It is therefore possible to have form without matter, because something that is complete and therefore cannot change further must be pure form.

Where change is explained as the insertion of form into matter, there must be both a shapeless matter and form without matter, the first in order to avoid an infinite explanatory regress and the second in order to avoid an infinite explanatory deferral. In addition, therefore, to prime matter, there must also be a prime mover, a cause that moves everything else but isn't itself moved by anything but itself.

What kind of substantial form could such a prime mover be, and why should there be only one and not many of them? Given the diversity of entities and events in the world, why shouldn't we suppose there to be multiple sources of change? Why must completed form without matter ultimately be singular?

The reason is that if there were multiple dynamics, they would form a set and not an individual, and where there is a set, there would be variation between the members of the set. In turn, variation implies divergence from the definition, divergence from definition implies incompleteness, incompleteness indicates the necessity of change, and the necessity of change implies that there is composition of matter and form, and not form without matter. Ultimately, therefore, singularity must follow from the requirement for completeness.

To achieve unity there must be both vertical and horizontal integration. What is meant by vertical integration? In my example, the thread is formed for the sake of the cloth and the cloth for the sake of the garment. But then you might ask, for the sake of what is the garment produced? And if it is to protect the wearer from the weather, for the sake of what is the wearer to be protected from the weather? One might answer to this that it is to support their wellbeing. Vertical integration refers to this hierarchy of final causes.

There are many such vertical hierarchies. As well as thread, cloth and garments, we also have, for example, timber, planks and furniture, and clay, bricks and buildings. Secondly, therefore, there has to be horizontal integration. Something must connect together all these explanatory chains and ensure that a vertical relation such as *thread–cloth–garment* is integrated not only with the relations *timber–plank–furniture* and *clay–brick–building* but also every other vertical relation. What is the *telos* that is common to garments, furniture, and buildings? To avoid an infinite deferral of explanation, and to complete both vertical and horizontal unification, the stack of explanation must end in something which integrates these diverse chains of explanation. What would be the characteristics of such a primary form which provides unity to the whole structure?

Firstly, this primary substance must be eternal, otherwise change would be contingent, not necessary; the entry in the *Stanford Encyclopedia of Philosophy* cites this passage from the *Metaphysics*:

> ...anything that is capable of being is also capable of not being. What is capable of not being might possibly not be, and what might possibly not be is perishable. Hence anything with the mere potentiality to be is perishable. What is eternal is imperishable, and so nothing that is eternal can exist only potentially – what is eternal must be fully actual. But the eternal is prior in substance to the perishable. For the eternal can exist without the perishable, but not conversely, and that is what priority in substance amounts to.

That is to say, in order for the cosmos to exist and keep turning, there must be a substance the form of which is actualisation. It must necessarily have no matter, because it has no potentiality, only actuality; otherwise there would be something else that was more complete. For the same reason, it must also be singular, because if there was more than one, then it would have matter: the existence of many instances of something implies the presence of matter as well as form.

What could move such a primary substance, since there is nothing towards which it is drawn? If it were to pay attention to something incomplete, it would be drawn towards incompleteness. Therefore, for the prime mover to be the ultimate object of attraction, it must be being drawn by itself; the object of its attention must be itself.

This establishes a link to cosmology and the requirement to map Aristotelian thinking to Christian doctrine. The geocentric model of the cosmos described in Ptolemy's *Almagest*, which was written in Egypt in the 2nd century, was a component of the synthesis of Aristotelian natural philosophy and Christian theology that prevailed in late middle ages, from the 12th to the 17th centuries. Terrestrial physics was assumed to be different from celestial physics, with each governed by its own principles. In Aristotle's cosmology, the 49 heavens move eternally in fixed circles within the outermost one, the primary heaven, which is moved by the prime mover. The movement of the primary heaven is drawn in the same way that a person is drawn to what they desire or what they want to understand, and it is the prime mover that is doing the drawing.

Aristotle considered theology the final and most important area of study and it is easy to see the affinity between the concept of a prime mover and the monotheistic conception of a creator. However, there were several questions that had to addressed to build a synthesis of Aristotelian natural philosophy with Christian doctrine. These questions concerned the creation, the existence and nature of God and the possibility of immortality. In general, the way these questions were resolved involved understanding the relationship of reason to faith.

The question of the creation follows from the Christian belief that the world was created by God *ex nihilo*, out of nothing, which is a clear contradiction to the Aristotelian ontology of eternal form and matter. There was no philosophical solution to this issue, and, in this context, appeal was made to the necessity for faith.

A second cause of contention was the issue raised by the Christian belief in the immortality of the soul and the resurrection of the body at the last judgement. The Aristotelian understanding that the soul is the form of the body militates against the possibility of personal survival after death, and Aristotle had no interest in such personal survival. If the soul is the form of the body, not a separate and separable component, how can this be accommodated within Christian doctrine.

This had also been a problem for Islamic commentators on Aristotle such as Ibn Rushd, known in Europe as Averroes. His solution was based on the very short, very opaque, chapter in *De Anima*, Aristotle's treatise on the soul in which Aristotle describes the idea of the active intellect.

Aristotle's conception of the soul, *psuche*, is much wider than the modern idea. The soul is the formal, efficient and final cause of a living organism. All living organisms have an animating principle which is their soul. This concept of a soul was inclusive: it encompasses the capacities for growth, reproduction and sustenance that are common to all living organisms; the capacities for sensation, perception and movement, which were attributable to both animals and human beings; and the capacity for intellect and rationality, which is attributable only to human beings.

Perception is the apprehension of the form of something without its matter. If perception were apprehension of both form and matter, sensation would be similar to nutrition, in the sense that what is external to the body is consumed in the process of apprehension. Perception is related to the sensory organs; eyes with vision, ears with sound and so on. The driver of perception is the form of the object perceived.

The intellect, on the other hand, isn't associated with any bodily component. There is both a passive and an active intellect. The passive intellect is concerned with forms apprehended in experience; in sensation, perception, and imagination. The idea of the active intellect is that it is the part of the intellect which is concerned with forms apprehended in conceptual thought and which can therefore be considered to be self-motivated, independent of the corporeal and the experiential. If the active intellect could be imagined as a separable component, then a path to the possibility of life after death was available.

In 13th century Europe, there was an Averroist party in this controversy. On the other hand, in Aquinas' thinking, represented in the *Summa Theologiae*, the view that the soul is the substantial form of the body doesn't undermine the view that human beings are a unity. So, although the rational capacity isn't perishable in the way the other capacities are, the intellect is not the soul and the soul is not the person and, therefore, the immortality of the soul would not be sufficient for the immortality of the person, because that also requires the resurrection of the body. The immortality of the soul and the resurrection of the body are therefore again questions of faith rather than arguable through philosophical reasoning.

A third issue was the question of the existence of God. While a variety of arguments were put forward, they tend to fall into three main types; ontological arguments, cosmological arguments and teleological arguments, or arguments from design.

Teleological arguments for the existence of God are arguments that start from observations of the structure and function of worldly objects in order to argue for the existence of a design and a designer. Cosmological arguments are arguments that start with the contingent nature of the world and argue that contingent existence requires a necessary existence, which is identified with God. The Aristotelian arguments for prime matter and a prime mover, that they are necessary to avoid an infinite regress of causes and an infinite deferral of objectives, are analogous to the cosmological argument.

An ontological argument for the existence of God was first put forward by Anselm of Canterbury in the 11th century. Interpretations differ with regard to exactly what the argument was, but it hinges on what might be called more generally the ontological principle, which is that ontology can be deduced from logic and that ontological necessity follows from logical necessity. The idea is to think of something which is the most complete of its kind where completeness includes actualisation. You then consider that, if that thing does not exist, something like it which does in fact exist would be even more complete. Since it is possible to imagine something that is complete, and existence is a component of completion, then what is imagined to be complete must also exist.

In the *Summa Theologiae*, Aquinas argued that there are five ways to demonstrate the existence of God. Three are versions of the cosmological argument. The first is that there cannot be an infinite deferral of final causes, the second that there cannot be an infinite regress of efficient causes, and the third is that at least one necessary being must exist because contingent beings have not always existed, and if everything were contingent, it would be possible for nothing to exist, because creation would be a contingent event.

The fourth way is a version of the ontological argument. Everything comes in degrees, including degrees of existence. Therefore, if there are entities which show degrees of completion, then it follows there must be something that exists that is complete. Behind this argument is the notion of plenitude; the idea that every station on the *scala naturae*, the ladder of being, must be occupied, including the ultimate station.

The fifth way is a version of the teleological argument: that everything in existence has a form and structure that fits it to a function and purpose. To avoid an infinite deferral again, there must be something which draws everything towards such a fulfilment without itself being drawn by something further.

These monotheistic arguments follow the pattern of Aristotle's argument for a prime mover to establish the necessity and the singularity of a god-like being. But the prime mover is not God, is not a creator, and has no interest in human beings. It is faith that builds the bridge that identifies this necessary being with a specific conception of God, of creation, and of human destiny.

How far arguments such as these go, and how far they were intended to go, is debated. Were they meant to convince a sceptic, or to provide a believer with a bridge from reason to faith? Interestingly, Aquinas' own argument against Anselm's version of the ontological argument is that it isn't possible for human beings to have a complete conception of God, only God can have that, so Anselm's argument would fail before the controversial move from conception to existence.

There are some characteristic features of the Aristotelian way of thinking. The first is what might be called a bias to belief. The idea underpinning this is that common belief, what was commonly known, had a basic level of reliability. Philosophical reflection started from what was learned first, what was simplest, and what was most widely believed. The approach is therefore weighted towards dialectic rather than critique. The method was to draw correct inferences from premises, where the premises are what was generally accepted by the most reliable sources. Underlying the method were indubitable premises, such as the principle of non-contradiction, which cannot be deduced from any more fundamental principle or proven, but which must be assumed if anything is to be thought and said at all.

Following the implications of these premises through to their logical conclusion often leads to puzzles or *aporia*. These puzzles are then investigated to see if they can be resolved. The process is dialectical in the sense that, starting from what is known, reflection inevitably turns up contradictions and differences of opinion. Then, through a kind of collaborative conflict, a resolution to these puzzles can be found. Knowledge advances through a continual repetition of this cycle.

The structure of education in Europe as it developed through this period was informed by this methodology. The process of education at the time was long and arduous. Each step prepared the student for the next step, so that the process was cumulative. The process of formation started with the trivium, which covered grammar, logic and rhetoric. Grammar built the ability to interpret language and texts, logic the ability to construct valid arguments and critique bad ones, and rhetoric the ability to deploy language to instruct and persuade. The trivium was followed by the quadrivium, which covered music, astronomy, arithmetic, and geometry, which were thought to be related disciplines concerned with different kinds of harmony and order. Together, the trivium and the quadrivium covered the seven liberal arts. The student would then go on to study Aristotelian natural philosophy, and, finally, enter the doctoral disciplines of medicine, law and theology.

The bias to belief was also the foundation of religious faith. Reason wasn't by itself sufficient to understand the existence and nature of God; these had to be understood through revelation, which meant either direct experience or the testimony of reliable sources regarding such experiences. Placing confidence in either of these implicitly means assuming a level of reliability in such experiences. The default assumption was to believe what one was experiencing, or the testimony of others regarding their experience, unless there was a reason not to.

This was recognised at the time as the distinction between natural philosophy and theology. Both disciplines are concerned with the same target domain, but natural philosophy considered only what could be inferred by demonstrative reason, whereas theology started from principles which were already believed and therefore depended on the possibility of reliable experience and reliable testimony.

One basis for this bias to belief was an underlying realism. The focus was on ontology and logic rather than epistemology because knowing wasn't understood to be fundamentally problematic in the way that it is today. Aristotle uses one and the same term for both the account that one can give of something and the organising principle of that thing: *logos*. Because experience and testimony were fundamentally reliable, the approach could also be empirical. Perception was the apprehension of substantial form through the senses. Rational intellect was the understanding of the relationships between substantial forms.

For this reason, ontology maps onto logic, so that the basic structure of reality, which is substance and property, has the same form as the basic structure of explanation, which is subject and predicate.

Philosophical realism is the idea that there is a fundamental level of congruence between the structure of reality and the structure of explanation, so that there is no fundamental gap between being and what is said about being, between the physical and the conceptual.

The synthesis of Aristotelian ontology and logic with Christian theology was largely constructed by the middle of the 14th century, but it continued to be expounded and taught into the 17th century. At the start of the 17th century the textbook version of the state of knowledge was still largely Aristotelian. It has been calculated that some 750 such textbooks were produced in the 15th century, and a further 6,653 between 1500 and 1650.

This gap between reality and explanation became an intellectual crisis in the Scientific Revolution of the 17th century, in Thomas Kuhn's sense that the anomalies that were being generated could no longer be ignored. However, the gap had started to open in the 14th century.

As I noted earlier, the identification of essences with universals in Aristotelianism was not straightforward. There are two reasons for this: firstly, universals apply to many entities, not just to one; and secondly, many universals apply to the same concrete individual entity, so which one captures its essence? They can't all do so, as that would contradict the idea of an essence. Why should the essence of something be what it has in common with many other things, rather than what makes it singular? A description such as *the solitary oak by the lake* intuitively appears to capture the substance of such an entity better than universals such as *oak*, *tree* or *plant*.

Over the next century or so, essentialism was challenged by two competing theories, which have been called conceptualism and nominalism. These were developed in the work of John Duns Scotus, William of Ockham, Jean Buridan and Nicole Oresme among others, with the tide moving away from realism without breaking out of the Aristotelian framework.

The problem with focusing the idea of form on universal predicates is that this doesn't explain the individuation of things. Duns Scotus, or his followers, introduced the idea that there was something real about the individuating attributes of entities. In the subject *this tree*, for example, the qualifier *this* referred to something substantial in the same way that the universal *tree* did. It captured the haecceity, the *thisness*, of an entity, while the universal captured its quiddity, its somethingness; literally its *whatness*.

William of Ockham argued that everything that exists is an individual. We have an apprehension of the type of an entity which is separate from our intuitive cognition of its existence. Cognitively, we intuit the existence of a separate entity before we abstractly recognise its type or form. Therefore, the reference of a concept is to the individuals that fall under the specification. Universal terms are the secondary intentions, that is the secondary targets, rather than the primary intentions of the apprehension of individual entities. Conceptual knowledge is then built on the basis of the assumption that there is a common course to nature, so that there are classes of individuals with common attributes, which can be the objects of knowledge.

Thomas Aquinas, Duns Scotus and William of Ockham were theologians and belonged to the new religious orders of their time, Aquinas a Dominican and the other two Franciscans. Like them, Jean Buridan taught at a university (he in Paris), but in logic and natural philosophy, not in theology. His approach was more empirical. In William of Ockham's conceptualism, universal terms were secondary to the conceptual structure. In his logic, Buridan paid close attention to the terms in which any discourse was actually carried out, arguing that rationality was a property of language. This meant that his approach was more obviously critical, because it interrogated the surface grammar to understand the deeper logic behind a discourse.

At the same time, there was a growing body of innovation in natural philosophy that challenged the Aristotelian thinking. In the field of physics, Buridan questioned the Aristotelian account of motion, suggesting that a thrown projectile, for instance, carried within it an impetus that had been transferred by the thrower in the act of throwing rather than it being drawn in the manner of a teleological explanation.

Nicole Oresme was also a master of arts at Paris, although he did complete his doctorate in theology. However, for the last twenty years of his life, he worked for king Charles V of France. Like Buridan, Oresme proposed alternatives to the Aristotelian conceptions of time and space. Where Aristotle had conceptualised time in terms of motion, Oresme proposed a conception of time as durations, and therefore prior to motion. Similarly, where Aristotle had considered that the place of a body was defined by the surrounding space, Oresme argued that the place of a body was the space it occupied.

27

In 1543 Nicolas Copernicus put forward a heliocentric model of the cosmos in a book called *On the Revolutions of the Celestial Spheres.* The Copernican model was mathematically simpler than the Ptolemaic model, but it didn't find easy acceptance because heliocentrism contradicted prevailing intuitions about the centrality of the Earth. In 1588 Tycho Brahe suggested a hybrid model in which he sought to reconcile the advantages of Copernicus' heliocentric model with Aristotelian physics. In this model, most of the planets revolve around the sun, which in turn revolves around the Earth, which therefore remained stationary, as it appears to do in experience.

Further anticipations of the new sciences can be found in works such as *De Rerum Natura* of Bernardino Telesio (published in 1586) and the *Novum Organum* of Francis Bacon (published in 1620). However, as Kuhn has suggested, paradigms are only replaced when there is a new paradigm available. In the absence of a plausible alternative, a framework of ideas can persist, even when its details are being questioned. The critiques of Buridan and Oresme were questions of the detail, not overall structure. What was missing was an alternative paradigm.

Brahe's hybrid model was the compromise in place in the early 17th century when observations made using the newly invented telescope became possible. This led to Galileo's discovery of four moons orbiting Jupiter in 1610, the event that can plausibly be regarded as the beginning of the Scientific Revolution, and the news of which resonated across Europe.

This is because these astronomical observations served in a very public fashion to undermine the distinction between the Earth and the heavens that was central to Aristotelian cosmology. The implication was that if there were only one kind of physical structure, there would only need to be one kind of analysis of motion, and one kind of physics to give an account of it. Hannah Arendt, in her book *The Human Condition*, identified the invention of the telescope, and its inverse the microscope, as one of the three events that were determinative of the modern world, alongside the Reformation and Europe's discovery of the New World.

The invention of the telescope and microscope were arguably the most revolutionary because they demonstrated that human perception was not necessarily adequate to understanding how things really worked. The structure of the universe could no longer be taken to be accessible without the aid of instrumentation, calling into question the assumption on which the Aristotelian synthesis was based, which was that the essence of things could be captured by observation.

Hylomorphism could be both realist and empiricist. However, as a consequence of the new technologies and discoveries, it became increasingly apparent that either the realism or the empiricism of Aristotelian thinking would have to be dropped. Over the next 150 years there was what might be thought of as a rear-guard attempt to keep the realism at the expense of empiricism, but, by the end of the 18th century, it would be the empiricism that prevailed and the realism that had to be abandoned. The next two sections cover these developments.

3. The Scientific Revolution

In the Aristotelian synthesis, natural philosophy was an integrated discipline: metaphysics was concerned with the principles of being; physics with the principles of nature; and the study of living organisms with the principles of life and the mind. The principles of life and the mind rested on the principles of physics, and the principles of physics on the principles of metaphysics. The re-fashioning of the cosmos by Copernicus, Johannes Kepler and Galileo brought the principles of physics into question, which inevitably meant that the other components were bought into question also, creating the need for a new way of thinking.

Galileo was an experimental physicist as well as a theoretical one. He differed from his predecessors in the sense that his concern was not so much to provide a model of the system that would be useful for making predictions, but to explain what was actually happening.

He argued that the book of nature was written in the language of mathematics. In his polemical *Dialogue Concerning the Two Chief World Systems*, which appeared in 1632, the argument clearly favours the Copernican over the Ptolemaic system. It was also clear that the new system was intended as a model of the way the heavens actually were, and it was this, rather than heliocentrism as such, which bought him into conflict with the Counter-Reformation and the institutions of the Church.

It had long been recognised that Ptolemy's model of the cosmos only approximated the circular motion posited in the theoretical cosmology of Aristotle, and relied on levels of complication and artifice to retain an approximate utility. It served its purpose in the sense that its predictions were reasonably reliable, without it being necessary to suppose that it was correct in some more literal way. It was an aid to calculation that could be said to *save the appearances*, but should not be taken to be a true account of the heavens.The same argument was deployed by cardinal Bellarmine against Galileo; supposing that the earth orbits the sun in order to make accurate and verifiable predictions doesn't demonstrate that the earth actually does orbit the sun, and for this reason, isn't sufficient to outweigh the evidence derived from the early church fathers exegisis of the Scriptures.

Galileo's final work was called the *Discourses and Mathematical Demonstrations Relating to Two New Sciences* and was published in 1638. It was the culmination of his project to create a science of mechanics and provide a mathematical description of matter and motion, which he had begun in the 1590s. The first new science was concerned with the cohesion of materials, with how stuff sticks together and resists being broken apart. The second was concerned with the principles of motion that would characterise the movement of both celestial and terrestrial bodies, describing both in a uniform and universal language. Galileo didn't complete a projected third part, concerned with collisions and what happens when one body impacts another.

In order to provide a mathematical description of matter, Galileo treats it as continuous. By reducing problems to questions of how levers, balances and pendulums function, he could demonstrate mathematically how bits of matter solidify and stick together, and how they break apart.

René Descartes was among the first to seek to provide not only a complete replacement for Aristotelian physics but also an alternative metaphysics. Descartes was circumspect about directly challenging prevailing ideas, suppressing his own earlier works on physics when he learned of the condemnation of Galileo until he was confident that he had a metaphysics with which to support them. The *Meditations on First Philosophy* was published in 1642, and the *Principles of Philosophy*, which explained his physics, followed in 1644.

Descartes conjectured that the planets orbited the sun carried by a medium whose rotations generated vortices, and that gravitational force was due to these vortices. Similarly, magnetism was due to corkscrew-shaped particles emitted at the Earth's poles, and magnetic polarity was explained by the direction of the thread.

In Descartes' view, space is not a container for matter, but simply the extent occupied by it. Matter has only the properties of size, shape, position and motion, and it is infinitely divisible, so there is no void. Because all motion is the result of impacts, there is no need to postulate action at a distance. Descartes proposed no principles of motion as such, suggesting that motion is determined and sustained by God. The question of how this infinitely divisible substance could cohere into individual entities was not resolved either. Why do these objects not simply drift apart on contact with something larger?

With regard to living organisms, Descartes argued that only human beings had souls. Metabolism, growth, reproduction and sensation were mechanical processes, in humans and in animals, as were behavioural responses to hazards and opportunities. The soul was concerned with intellect and will and therefore with what was consciously experienced, including memory and imagination.

Descartes' metaphysical ontology posited the existence of three substances, each of which had a single defining attribute. God is the only true substance, because the only entity that is not dependent on anything else. Created substances are sustained only through God's concurrence, and there are two kinds of them, matter and mind. In the Cartesian system, substances remain the independent category, while the other Aristotelian categories become modes of substances.

The essence of matter is extension in three dimensions. In addition to size, shape, position and motion, matter also has the properties of existence and duration. Because matter is continuous, there can be an infinite number of extended material substances through division.

The essence of mind is thought. Minds have two capacities, intellect and will. Like matter, they also have existence and duration, but they don't have extent, so minds are singular. Intellect is divided into pure intellect, on the one hand, and imagination and perception on the other. While intellect is independent of the body, imagination and perception are dependent on it. The mind also has volition, comprising desires, aversions and states of belief and doubt that are grounded in the intellectual faculty. A human being is therefore a composite of multiple extended substances and a single thinking substance. This substance dualism of matter and mind immediately raises the problem of how these two are meant to interact, a problem to which Descartes didn't really have a solution, though he did suggest that perhaps the interface was in the pituitary gland.

Before he was ready to propose his new ontology, Descartes made his arguments on the empirical grounds of simplicity and scope. The simplicity stemmed from the few basic modes of substance, and the scope flowed from the fact that explanations extended to all terrestrial and celestial phenomena.

For particular phenomena, we are reliant on observation, measurement and counting, activities that can only be done empirically. Practical knowledge is also empirical, and usually sufficient for its purposes. However, in his first principles, Descartes argued that the essences of substances weren't accessible to the senses. To access these, it was necessary to *withdraw the mind from the senses* and lean instead on innate ideas, which can be clearly and distinctly known. The foundational argument *I think, therefore I am* was such a clear and distinct idea. The principles of mathematics could also be grasped in the same way. One consequence of this confidence in intuition was that the principles of the intellect could be known with certainty while empirical evidence was always subject to error and correction.

Where did this certainty come from? Descartes relies on the ontological proof of the existence of God to argue that we can be confident in clear and distinct ideas: if we couldn't, it would imply that God was a deceiver, and no perfect being could be a deceiver.

Although Descartes' methodology was the method of doubt, it is not real doubt, because the underlying epistemology was built on the bias to believe.

Descartes' thinking addressed the fundamental epistemological challenge that the new sciences posed. The Aristotelian concept of substantial form permitted the congruence of an empirical epistemology with an essentialist ontology because substantial form was accessible to the senses. The phenomenal form of a tree, a horse or a bridge was congruent with its substantial form. That meant that rational thought could start from the appearance of things and work forward from there through the processes of reasoning. This process would generate puzzles, *aporia*, which could then be resolved through demonstrative arguments. If what is perceived through the senses is only the appearance of things, and appearance differs from essence, then this procedure becomes much less compelling.

The new sciences opened up a gap between primary attributes and secondary attributes. Primary attributes could be measured and counted and could be said to be in the object that was the target of cognition. Secondary attributes were how things appeared to an observer; they were the product of an interaction between subject and object and therefore raised the question of what was happening in the subject of cognition, a concern that hadn't been salient before.

Descartes' physics, though very influential for a century, was abandoned in the 18th century. Both his ontology and his epistemology depended on the existence of God to keep the wheels turning and to underwrite the mind's intuitions, and both foundered on contradictions and incoherence. Outside mathematics, Descartes' most lasting legacy was to move the most significant dividing line between entities from the distinction between the living and the non-living to the distinction between mind and body.

In the early 17th century, there was little in the way of an institutional structure to science. The universities were dominated by scholasticism. The first scientific society was the Accademia dei Lincei, the 'academy of lynxes', established in 1603. Galileo was the sixth member, joining in 1611 after his discovery of the moons of Jupiter. The contemporary scientific community was an extended network of personal contacts and correspondents. Descartes, Pierre Gassendi and Thomas Hobbes were all within the circle around Marin Mersenne, who had been a student with Descartes at the Jesuit college of La Flèche in Anjou, and it was through this channel that Gassendi and Hobbes contributed their objections to Descartes' *Meditations*. One advantage of such informal networks of correspondents is that women, at least well-connected women, could be part of the network at a time when women were excluded from formal institutional structures.

In the 17th century two versions of the mechanical theory were proposed. In Descartes' version matter was continuous and there were no voids. The other version *was the atomic hypothesis*. Atomism had been first proposed by Democritus of Abdera, a contemporary of Socrates, and had later been taken up by the Stoics and the Epicureans. Gassendi and Hobbes were the principal proponents of the atomic hypothesis at this time. The atomic hypothesis proposed that there were voids between the particles of matter through which they moved.

Like Galileo, Gassendi was both a theoretical and experimental physicist, conducting experiments in astronomy, optics and mechanics. He argued for an empirical approach to science and philosophy, though not to theology, although much of his own work did not actually live up to this standard. The empirical approach recognised that substance is not accessible because it cannot be perceived through the senses. The senses disclose only how things appear to us, not how they might be in their own definition. At the same time, while rejecting any form of foundationalism, Gassendi also rejected sceptical arguments to the effect that knowledge was not possible at all. Empirical evidence had confirmatory value. While our senses are not wholly reliable, nor are they completely unreliable. Gassendi allows for indirect inference from what is observable as a means of gaining knowledge of what is unobservable. One consequence of this is that we cannot know with certainty anything grasped empirically.

In opposition to Descartes, Gassendi does not regard God as functioning to guarantee human intuitions. He also rejects the ontological argument on the basis that existence isn't an attribute of something but a pre-condition of its being something.

The Cartesian view was that matter is continuous and infinitely divisible, and space and time are simply the extents occupied by matter. Gassendi supported the atomic theory which, in contrast, proposes that space and time are absolutes and that matter is built up from indivisible particles of varying shapes, sizes, solidity and weight. In this perspective, it is weight that generates motion. Basic atoms combine to form larger aggregates, of which the large-scale entities of the familiar world are in turn comprised. It is the greater activity of some kinds of atom that gives rise to more complex structures such as living organisms.

This contest between realists and empiricists that Descartes and Gassendi exemplified persisted into the second half of the 17th century. Gassendi's views were received more positively in England than in France, where the Cartesian approach prevailed, and among the leading figures in this second generation were John Locke and Isaac Newton, along with Newton's rival Gottfried Wilhelm Leibniz.

By the second half of the century the institutional form of scientific activity had become better established. The Royal Society in London was set up in 1660 and counted among its original members, along with Newton and Locke, luminaries such as Robert Boyle, Edmund Halley, Robert Hooke and Christopher Wren. Similar organisations were established in Paris in 1666 and in Berlin in 1700 and would proliferate in the following century. These organisations had a commitment to empirically driven science and experiment.

Newton's major work, the *Principia Mathematica*, was published in 1687. He argued that observation and experiment should not only function to confirm a hypothesis but should also be the sole basis for its formulation. In his rules of reasoning, he argued that propositions gathered from observing phenomena should be accepted unless other phenomena serve to strengthen or weaken them and not because they were contradicted by a contrary hypothesis. Results should be taken from well-designed experiments and mathematical theories constructed to draw inferences from them. Where there was an absence of empirical data on the basis of which to draw inductive inferences, the method should be not to advance through speculation, but to hold off until more information is available.

John Locke's *Essay Concerning Human Understanding,* which was published two years later in 1689, was perhaps the first response to the new physics which didn't start from the assumption that the world was entirely knowable. Locke was first of all concerned with what it might be possible for human beings to know – that is, with the limits of human understanding and the horizon of human knowledge.

Locke argued against the possibility of innate knowledge, claiming that the human mind should be considered a blank slate. His argument was that if ideas were innate, then children would have them, but this doesn't seem to be the case. One possible counter-argument was that such innate ideas were there but were only perceived under certain conditions. Locke's answer to this was that this could apply to any idea, which made it possible that all ideas might be innate, or – and this was the more likely hypothesis – that none were. Locke also rejected the idea that truth could be inferred from common assent, pointing out that ideas differ across times and cultures. The target of these arguments was the basic premises of Aristotelian thinking, but they apply also to the arguments of Descartes and Leibniz.

Like the Aristotelians, Locke thought that everything in the mind begins in the senses. From the senses we learn about the external world and from reflection on this information we can learn about the workings of our own minds. The mind cannot create simple ideas, which must come through the sense, but it can combine them into complex ones. These complex ideas are of three kinds: modes or attributes can be associated with substances; the congruence of related ideas can be established; and general ideas that can apply to a whole population of objects can be created by abstraction from individual instances of that population.

Like Gassendi, Locke adhered to the atomic hypothesis. The material world was composed of atoms in motion in a void. Atoms have the primary qualities of extent, shape, solidity and motion. They also have secondary qualities, which are evident in the way they look and feel to an observer. It was not clear to Locke what the link was between primary and secondary qualities, whether or not one caused the other, and how far we can infer anything about unobservable primary qualities from observable secondary ones.

This creates a difficulty around the concept of substance. In keeping with the tradition, Locke thought substances (such as God, angels, humans, animals, plants, and human artefacts) existed independently, while modes were dependent on substances. In contrast to substances, modes are creations of the active mind. Locke distinguished simple modes from mixed modes. Modes correspond to concepts and are constructions that we use as a standard or baseline to make sense of the world.

Substances must exist in order for there to be modes, because modes must be modes of something. But what is a substance if it is an unobservable? Locke calls it an *I know not what*. In this way, Locke drew a distinction between the real essence of things, which was their atomic construction, and the nominal essence of things, which is the way they appear to us. Our complex ideas of trees and horses and bridges pick out the nominal essence of things; but the organising principle in nature, according to the atomic hypothesis, is matter in motion, and this is the basis of their real essence. Regarding the extent to which real essence can be inferred from nominal essences, Locke seems to have thought that there was a connection and that, even if we begin with confused ideas, criticism in the light of continuing experience will tend to see nominal essences converge on real essences.

Knowledge for Locke is *the perception of the connexion and agreement or disagreement and repugnancy of any of our ideas.* Different forms of knowledge merit different levels of confidence. The highest level of confidence is secured by the modal knowledge of our own concepts. The second highest level of confidence pertains to what can be inferred by demonstrative reasoning, such as the existence of God, but we can only have probabilistic knowledge of ultimate reality. Probability in this context is not the mathematical concept of probability, but is concerned with the validity of testimony, where the relevant criteria are things like the credibility of witnesses and the cumulative strength of the evidence.

From the traditional Aristotelian perspective, the concept of substance answered the question of identity. However, Locke's substance, the *I know not what*, will not function in the same way, and this led him to re-formulate the concept of personal identity. Identity is generally founded on two ideas connected to location in space and time: exclusion and continuity. Exclusion means that only one thing can occupy any given location, and continuity means that a single thing can only ever be at one location. Atoms have identity in this sense and persist through time. Physical systems, which are collections of atoms, don't have this identity, because their components are continually being added to and subtracted from. Living organisms, on the other hand, are distinguished by their organisation rather than their composition, and the identity through time of a living organism is grounded in the continuity of this organising principle rather than through material composition.

However, exclusion applies only to similar kinds, so a soul and a body can be co-located. Locke distinguishes between the human being and the person. The human being was the living organism while the person was grounded in continuity of consciousness through time. This was a new idea at the time. Consciousness was the concept of self-awareness, the mind's capacity to reflect on its own operation and experience happiness and suffering. Continuity of consciousness is the awareness of being the same self at different times and places. Consciousness was not the same thing as soul; it was the content of the mind, whereas the soul was the functioning.

Personal immortality required continuity of consciousness in order that the judgement in the afterlife reflected the merits of the life lived, and so that a person could then take responsibility for their actions in the present life. *Person* is therefore for Locke a forensic term. We think about what we are going to do because we understand that we will be held responsible for it, and similarly, we can understand sanctions and punishments as the consequence of our actions.

Without these conditions, any concept of justice, including divine justice, would lose its meaning.

Locke had come to the conclusion that substance, the central concept of the Aristotelian tradition, was an *I know not what*; substances, if they existed, were beyond the horizon of human understanding. His near contemporary Leibniz also accepted the mechanical model in physics, but did not share Locke's willingness to accept such a horizon. In his view, the mechanical model of the new sciences wasn't complete because it lacked final causes, and if there weren't final causes in physics, the implication was that these must be found in metaphysics, and more particularly in the central metaphysical concept of substance. Where Locke's project was a new map of the horizon of human understanding in the light of the new physics, Leibniz' project was to reconcile the new physics with traditional metaphysics, and the results can be seen to underline the challenges of such a project.

Leibniz developed a theory of *monads* or simple substances. Monads aren't themselves material and they have no spatial extension, but they manifest themselves through the body in which they are present. Monads don't interact with each other. Every monad is a world apart and evolves according to an internal dynamic. A monad has a point-of-view on the universe, and each one represents the entire universe from this particular point-of-view. In aggregate, monads represent all the possible perspectives on the universe, and, for this reason, they are therefore God's perspective on the world.

Physical structures and systems, composed of matter in motion, are phenomena derived from the perceptual state of monads. Their reality is grounded in the diachronic coherence of a monad as it unfolds through time and the synchronic coherence between monads. This alignment is a harmony pre-established by God.

Monads are independent of everything except God. How then do events happen? How do we explain, in Leibniz' own example, an historical event such as Alexander the Great's conquest of Persia and the defeat of Darius, if there is no connection between them? Surely the one being the vanquisher and the other the vanquished are historical contingencies. Leibniz' answer is that all events in a life are a part of its definition. It is the pre-established harmony that ensure that, when Alexander invades Persia, the events in the life of Alexander and the events in the life of Darius dovetail. Pre-established harmony also explains why the actions of someone's body appear to co-ordinate with the actions of their mind, so the intention to move is accompanied by an actual movement.

This harmony is not maintained by any connection between monads, which are worlds apart and don't interact - Leibniz says that they are 'windowless' - nor is it due to divine intervention from time to time, a theory called occasionalism. It is a harmony that flows from the perfection of the original creation, in the way that two perfect pendulums set swinging at the same time will remain in harmony although there is no connection between them.

One consequence of this pre-established harmonisation is that we can give two different explanations of why something is happening.

We can consider either final causes, which are connected to the mind, or efficient causes, which are connected to matter. The same event can be explained either in mechanical terms, following mathematical principles, or in ethical terms, following moral principles, and these explanations will be complementary.

Monads are organised into hierarchies. A living organism is a composite of many monads, each represented by a particular structure or system within the organism. At the base of the hierarchy, there are a set of infinitely small primitive components. Monads are composed of perceptions and appetites. In the hierarchy of monads, the dominant monads at the top of the hierarchy have clearer and more distinct perceptions, while the simpler monads at the bottom have the most confused perceptions. The hierarchy of containment is therefore also a hierarchy of relative clarity or confusion of perceptions.

In every composite entity, there is a dominating monad that gives the whole its identity. In an animal, the dominant monad has a capacity for sentience. The monad that is dominant in the collection of monads that is a human being has the capacity for what Leibniz calls *apperception*, or the awareness of its own perceptions and appetites. That is, it possesses a capacity for reflection.

It could be asked: if monads mirror the entire universe from a particular point-of-view, and some monads such as human beings have the capacity for self-reflection, why aren't human beings aware of everything that will ever happen in the universe? To answer this question, Leibniz posited the concept of *petites perceptions*, perceptions so minute that the mind is not aware of them, in the way that we don't hear the individual waves when we stand on a beach, but only the aggregate sound of the swell.

The relationship between higher-level and lower-level monads is one of dominance and subordination. One monad is dominant over another when it contains within it the reasons for the actions of the subordinate monads. In the case of human being, for instance, the monad that is the mind is at the top of the hierarchy of monads and contains within it the reasons for the functioning of every subordinate component within the entity.

Between different types of entity, this hierarchy of monads maps to the *scala naturae*, the ladder of being, starting with simple monads at the bottom, which look like stones and raindrops, continuing though plants, then animals, human beings, immaterial beings such as angels, and culminating in God. Leibniz doesn't subscribe to Descartes' strict ontological distinction between mind and matter; rather he posits a graduated hierarchy. This principle of continuity is one of the building blocks of his thinking.

How did Leibniz get to the theory of monads? His reasoning for the necessary existence of simple substances, and the necessity of them having the characteristics they do, is described in his *Monadology*. Leibniz thought that the mechanical model of physics lacked completeness. It could explain in mechanical terms how a given structure or system functioned, but not why it existed, except by invoking another mechanical structure or system. There were no final causes. However, at the same time, it was no longer tenable simply to maintain the Aristotelian view of substantial form.

In the Aristotelian synthesis, logic is closely coupled to ontology. The concept of a substance in ontology mapped to the concept of a subject in logic. Leibniz argued that, when an assertion is true, the concept of the predicate is contained in the concept of the subject. For anything to be a substance, therefore, it must have a complete individual concept, a concept that contains every possible applicable predicate whether past, present and future. Such a concept must include not only every possible universal that identifies the type of something, its *somethingness*, but also every possible particular that identifies its *thisness*, the haecceity of an individuated entity.

The complete individual concept of a *this something* contains everything that describes its *thisness* and everything that describes it's *somethingness*, not only now, but at all times. This implies that a substance will contain not only the marks of everything that has happened to it and everything that will happen to it but also the traces of everything that has happened in the universe throughout time. In order for a substance to mirror the entire universe in this way, substances must have appeared in the creation and will have to endure until the end of time. Substances must therefore be souls, because only souls are imperishable, and therefore, by extension, substances must be selves.

Furthermore, only substances can be active, and this activity must originate internally. Activity must therefore be the evolution of perceptions and appetites, as perceptions and appetites are the only contents of substances. It also follows that because substances map to a complete individual concept which is unchanging, substances must be a unity: they cannot be divided or joined, and there cannot be causal interactions between them. It follows that the interconnections between phenomenal interactions that are empirically observable must be due to something else, which is the reason why a pre-established harmony is invoked.

In addition to the principle of continuity, there are five other principles that anchor Leibniz's thinking. These are the principles of predicate-in-notion, the principle of sufficient reason, the principle of the identity-of-indiscernibles, the principle of contradiction and the principle of the best. These are not principles that can be arrived at empirically. They are innate ideas that can be established by analysis of the concepts involved. Leibniz pictured innate ideas existing in the mind in the way that veins structure the interior of a block of marble, creating a pre-formation from which necessary truths can be derived. The possibility of necessary truth is a corollary of the principle of contradiction.

The principle of the predicate-in-notion is the idea that every substance has a complete individual concept. It is the foundation of Leibniz's thinking about monads. Every substance must have a complete individual concept, and in order to be individual each substance must be different. Each individuated entity must be unique because the principle of sufficient reason would supply no reason for the creation of duplicates. If two entities were identical, there wouldn't be a sufficient reason for one to exist and not the other. Leibniz doesn't mean here that entities are always distinguishable by relationships in space and time, he means by their interior attributes. The principle of sufficient reason in turn follows from the idea of the complete individual concept, because if there were a truth that had no reason, then there would be a concept of a subject which didn't contain the concept of the predicate.

The principle of the identity-of-indiscernibles is a corollary of both the principle of the predicate-in-notion and the principle of sufficient reason. The principle of the identity-of-indiscernibles is the basis of Leibniz's rejection both of atoms in physics and the conception of the soul as a *tabula rasa*. In both cases, if these were possible, then there would be multiple identical entities, violating the principle of the identity-of-indiscernibles.

Finally, the principle of the best is a corollary of the principle of sufficient reason. It is the basis of Leibniz's optimism. This principle holds that rational beings always act for the best, because moral goodness provides a sufficient reason for action. Although human minds can only act for the best within the limitations of their own knowledge, God will always act for the best with complete knowledge, so that everything that happens must be for the best in this the best of all possible worlds. Voltaire mercilessly satirised this conclusion in the character of Doctor Pangloss in *Candide*.

By the end of the 17th century, the contours of the contention between realism and empiricism had started to come into focus. Conceptual structures map to the observable world. They are how we make sense of it. In the Aristotelian model, the observable world was the real functionable world. The invention of the telescope and the microscope had shown that the observable world was only a part of the real world, and might not be the functional component at unobservable scales. Locke had accepted this possibility, and captured it in the distinction between the real essence and the nominal essence of things.

Leibniz, on the other hand, while recognising that the old metaphysics was untenable, didn't accept the loss of final causes that this implied. His solution was to develop the idea of the complete individual concept and the monad. Entities were collections of monads and events the evolution of monads in time. In this way, the connection between conceptual structure and physical structure was preserved and the real essence and the nominal essence of things could be unified.

4. The Enlightenment

The dominant dynamic of the 18th century Enlightenment was a movement to replace authority with reason. Reason was not expected to overturn traditional ideas but to give them a rational foundation. However, it became clearer over time that instead of re-grounding traditional ideas such as the existence of God and the immortality of the soul on more secure foundations, rational enquiry could easily end up undermining them.

The Enlightenment's centre of gravity was in France. In terms of unfinished business, there was firstly the question of resolving the contest between Cartesian and Newtonian physics. One empirical test was the Newtonian prediction that the Earth should be flatter at the poles than at the equator; that the Earth was a flattened sphere. In 1736, two Geodesic Missions were sponsored by king Louis XV of France with the objective of measuring the length of an arc of the meridian. One headed north to Lapland, the second south to Ecuador. The second was beset by problems and only confirmed its result in 1739; the first, led by Pierre Louis Maupertuis, an advocate of Newton's theory, was able to report that that the Earth was indeed flattened at the poles, effectively ending the argument in the Newtonian's favour.

During the 18th century the Newtonian system was developed into the paradigm of classical mechanics. Prominent among the many works whereby this was achieved were Leonhard Euler's book *Mechanica*, published in 1736, and Pierre-Simon Laplace's multi-volume *Mécanique céleste*, published between 1799 and 1825.

While Newton was taken to have confirmed the heliocentric model of the solar system, there were still details to be confirmed. If the Earth orbits the sun, a star's apparent angle when observed from a particular location will vary between spring and autumn, as the Earth's orientation relative to the sun is reversed between these two times, and as it is either moving towards the star or away from it. These phenomena are called stellar parallax and stellar aberration. The first measurement of stellar aberration was made by James Bradley in 1725; stellar parallax was not observed until the work of Friedrich Bessel in 1838.

A second strand in the Enlightenment was the circle around Denis Diderot and Jean d'Alembert, the editors and publishers of the *Encyclopédie*, which appeared between 1751 and 1766. They also wrote many of the entries. The target of this strand of the Enlightenment movement was in the first instance the French state and church. The thinking was that, if rational enquiry is open to everyone, what purpose did the hierarchies of the *ancien régime* serve – other than as a support for irrationality and superstition?

There was also a centre of Enlightenment thinking in Scotland, where David Hume, Adam Smith and Joseph Black were leading figures. One objective of the work of David Hume was to bring the Newtonian method to bear on the study of human nature, foregoing speculation and *a priori* assumptions about subjects that weren't accessible to human understanding in favour of experience and observation of what was. Like Locke, Hume pursued a critical project in order to determine the limits of reason and construct an empirical science of human nature. Hume wanted to find an ideally small set of principles, analogous to Newton's laws of motion in physics, that would explain how the mind worked.

Hume divided the contents of the mind, which he called perceptions, into impressions and ideas. Impressions include sensations, emotions and desires, and ideas are the images of these in reflection. Impressions can be generated in reaction to ideas. Both impressions and ideas can be simple or complex. Simple ideas are copies of simple impressions, which can be combined into complex ideational compositions. In this context, simplicity means that there no component parts into which the idea or impression can be analysed, whereas complexity means that the object can be broken down into simpler components.

The content of ideas is determined by their definitions. Starting from the terms used, the associated idea is determined. If the idea is complex, it can be broken down into its simplest components, and then these simple ideas can be connected to the simple impressions from which they originate in order to discover their cognitive content.

The association of ideas is for Hume what gravitational force is for Newtonian physics, serving as the basic principle of his account of the mind. It is the basic connection between ideas. There are three principles of association: resemblance, contiguity and causation. These are the basis of our conception of the universe.

Hume's view is that much of metaphysics lacks any real content. He challenged the possibility of knowledge of necessary connections through demonstrative reasoning. Demonstrative reasoning proceeds from first premises to conclusions, and the reasoning demonstrates how the conclusion must follow from the premises. Geometry in the style of Euclid was the model and Spinoza's *Ethics,* as an example of this approach, was laid out in the form of a treatise in geometry.

Hume followed Locke in analysing the limits of probable knowledge. He divided objects of reasoning into relations of idea and matters of fact. *A priori,* demonstrative knowledge was concerned with relations of ideas and was independent of the state of the world. Matters of fact, on the other hand, reflected the state of the world, and could not be arrived at by demonstrative reasoning or established with certainty. Facts were not necessarily true because the contrary state was always possible.

For the same reason, causal connections weren't necessary connections, as it was possible, without contradiction, to conceive of the effect not being followed the cause. Causation is the association that links past and present experiences to expectations for the future. If causal inferences weren't necessary connections, then they must be matters of fact. Hume concluded that causal relations are based on the experience of the repetitive conjunction of events. Causal reasoning is therefore probable reasoning from the conjunction of events, supported by an idea of the uniformity of nature, which was itself a probabilistic idea. This meant that our beliefs about cause and effect are based on custom and habit and flow from human nature. What had previously been considered necessary connections by philosophers were actually a felt determination of the mind based on an associative connection made in the mind, meaning that necessary connection was a construction in the mind of an observer.

As a target of observation, the definition of a cause from the external point-of-view was an event, followed by another, where all the events similar to the first are followed by events similar to the second. In parallel, from the internal point-of-view, a cause is a mental object whose appearance in the mind leads to the appearance in the mind of a second mental object.

These developments, nor surprisingly, had ethical and political ramifications. Hume's empiricist skepticism undermined not only ideas about necessary connection in nature but also necessary connection in personal identity. If a person was not an integrated individual, there must be some other way of being a person.

Leibniz had argued for a kind of complementarity between the newly emerging scientific account of events and the traditional human experience of the same events. The scientific account was concerned with efficient causes and the reasons why one thing followed from another, whereas human experience was concerned with final causes and the purposes for the sake of which events happened. A pre-established harmony established by God meant that these two accounts aligned.

In Hume's argument, there is also a congruence between events of cause and effect in the external world and the relation in the mind between the idea of the cause and the idea of the effect. The alignment between event and idea is a consequence of the associative functioning of the mind working on empirical impressions through custom and habit and observing a natural world in which a reasonable level of uniformity holds.

One significant difference between these two conceptions is that whereas Hume believes in a reasonable level of uniformity in nature supporting an association of ideas, Leibniz believed that the external world is organised around necessary connections which map to the necessary connections of reason. The armature of this organisation in nature are the principle of sufficient reason and the idea of a complete individual concept, from which follows a requirement for the identity-of-indiscernibles. From this it also follows that the subject–predicate relation in logic is always a necessary connection, however historically contingent the relationship might appear to be.

Immanuel Kant was educated in a tradition heavily influenced by Leibniz but moderated by the influence of the empiricists Locke and Hume and the developing Newtonian physics. Kant argued that we can have knowledge of the external world, not because it is organised according to substantial form or the principle of sufficient reason, or because the mind makes associations in the presence of a reasonable uniformity in nature, but because our understanding is a composite of content received through the senses and structure supplied by the mind.

The basic content of thought Kant calls *Anschauungen*, usually translated as *intuitions*. Space and time are pure – that is, non-empirical – intuitions that accompany and condition every sensible intuition, while experience is the origin of all empirical intuitions.

The mind has a number of functions, including representation, imagination and reasoning. The process is roughly as follows: sensations are turned into perceptions in the mind through the application of the pure intuitions of space and time and the conceptual structuring imposed by the categories of thought. There are twelve of these, divided into four groups: quantity, quality, modality and relation. In this model, substance and causality are components of the category of relation.

Perceptions are then conceptualised by the imagination through the application of schemata, which are a set of rules associated with each category. The application of these rules allows the mind to associate a universal term, a concept, with an individuated entity, to recognise something from its appearance as an instance of a type of entity (such as *bridge, tree* or *horse*) or of a type of event (such as *spanning, growing* or *grazing*). Concepts then form the basis of a judgement. A judgement is an association of a subject with a predicate in the form *X is y*, where *x* and *y* are concepts. In this way we make a judgement such as *The bridge is spanning the river* or *The horse is grazing in the field under the tree*. These judgements, which are at the apex of Kant's cognitive model, are made by the reason.

One consequence of this is the distinction between things as we understand them and things as they really are *an Sich*, or in themselves. There is a distinction between the noumenal, the real world which cannot be known, and the phenomenal, the appearance of things, which can. In Kant's view, scientific knowledge only extends to phenomena, and therefore the causal determinism of physics only applies to the phenomenal. The noumenal, in contrast, is free from this kind of determination. In addition to the things-in-themselves, the scope of the noumenal includes God and the self, and is the basis of freedom and immortality.

Contrary to Locke, Kant argued that the continuity of the self was a consequence of process rather than content, the process being the synthesis in the mind of representations, concepts and judgements. The continuity of self-awareness and the sense of personal identity through time come from an internal awareness of the continuity of these processes of synthesis. The mind in this view is necessarily active in synthesising judgements and therefore also necessarily aware of itself as the source of this activity.

One corollary of this self-awareness is the distinction between the objective and subjective. Kant argues that a self-aware mind makes the distinction based on the level of necessary connection between mental representations. For example, as you walk around a building, its appearance will change as your point-of-view changes. Are any judgements that you make about the building in the course of this walk objective or subjective? In order to identify that it is your point-of-view and not the building which is changing, you need to actively synthesise the representations from each point-of-view. If they fit together as a cohesive whole, you judge that these representations are indeed objective and that the judgement says something about the object. If they don't, you judge that the representations are subjective and the judgement is saying something about you, the observer.

What differentiates the human mind from other minds is the capacity to conceptualise mental representations and then synthesise judgements in these conceptual terms. The conceptual synthesis of concepts into judgements requires self-awareness. Self-awareness is necessary in order to make the judgement *I think that the appearance of this building is evolving because I am walking around it and my point-of-view is changing.* This is a necessary pre-condition of a recognition of the separation of thinker from thought.

The mind doesn't impose the categorial structure on the self, so the person, the *I* who is doing the reasoning, is free from the determination that is imposed on everything phenomenal. This means that the noumenal self, the self of moral thinking, is free from the constraints of the phenomenal world, and it is this insight that forms the basis of Kant's moral philosophy. Moral freedom is exercised through adherence to categorical imperatives, which are imperatives which are unconstrained by phenomenal constraints.

In Kant's argument for the existence of God, the immortality of the soul and the resurrection of the body are beliefs – justified beliefs – but not rationally demonstrable truths. The justification for holding these beliefs is that the disjunction of categorical imperatives that govern the noumenal self and the contingent imperatives that govern the phenomenal self could only be bridged over an extended timescale in a universe governed by divine providence.

Regarding the proofs of the existence of God, Kant argued that the cosmological argument and the argument from design depend on the ontological argument, and the ontological argument was unsound because existence isn't a predicate.

The argument here is that saying of anything that it exists doesn't add to the concept of the thing. Normally, an existential statement would be in the form *There is some object*. The negative existential statement, *There is no object*, only has meaning in some context, for example, *There is no object in the building.*

A classificatory statement, on the other hand, has the form *There is some object that satisfies the concept y* or, negatively, *There is no object that satisfies the concept y.* The first would apply if *y* means *bears* and the second if *y* means *dragons.* There is no need to say *There is some object that satisfies the concept exists*, since the first part of the sentence already says that. Equally, saying *There is some object that doesn't satisfy the concept exists* would be contradictory.

The problem is that in natural language both existential and classificatory statements have the same subject–predicate structure, and the two get conflated, so that we say *bears exist* and *dragons don't exist,* which appear to be attributing existence to bears and absence of existence to dragons.

However, if existence was a classificatory category, then there would be a population of *bears-that-exist* that exist, and another population of *bears-that-don't-exist* that don't exist, which is superfluous. It's worse in the case of dragons, where there is both a population of *dragons-that-exist* and a population of *dragons-that-don't-exist.* We could then say that *dragons-that-exist* don't exist, which is contradictory, but there doesn't appear to be any means of resolving the concept *dragons-that-don't-exist*, except to say either that *dragons-that-don't-exist* do exist, which is contradictory, or that *dragons-that-don't-exist* don't exist, which is redundant. In summary, existence isn't a fact about the *somethingness* of bears but that doesn't apply to the *somethingness* of dragons. It is instead a fact about the actualisation of bears which doesn't apply to dragons.

These arguments allowed Kant to provide an answer to the question concerning how there can be a correspondence between our conceptual representations and the external world. In the Aristotelian tradition, the order in rational thinking follows from the order in nature that is a consequence of substantial form. Leibniz attributed the congruence to a divinely established harmony, while Hume's argument implies an analogy between the associational functioning of the mind and an implied level of uniformity present in nature. Kant's answer is that the external world appears to be rule-governed in a way that we can understand because those rules have been imposed on our experience of it by the human mind. Our intuitions of space and time, together with the categories of thought and the schemata associated with them, are the necessary conditions of human cognition. The only way we can apprehend the world is on the basis of this rule-like regularity.

5. The scientific disciplines

During the first half of the 19th century, the most significant philosophical movement in Europe was German idealism, of which Georg Wilhelm Friedrich Hegel was the most influential exponent. Hegel's most trenchant opponent was Arthur Schopenhauer. Although Schopenhauer outlived Hegel by almost 30 years, his principal work *The World as Will and Representation* was published in 1818, just as Hegel took up the position as professor of philosophy at the University of Berlin, and they can be regarded as contemporaries.

In Leibniz' version of idealism, every entity has its complete individual concept and these are unchanging. In Aristotelianism, matter and form are different levels of completeness, where completeness is measured in terms of closeness to concept, and in the teleological conception of change, structures and systems evolve as they are drawn towards this state of completion.

The Hegelian dialectic, on the other hand, is a logic of position, opposition and reconciliation, sometimes described as the logic of thesis, antithesis and synthesis. The end-state is the elimination of all contradictions rather than closeness to concept. If it is partial and incomplete, a position generates an opposition, which is removed through a reconciliation, in which the contradictions are resolved, *aufgehoben*. The original components are not themselves removed, but raised up and preserved in the higher synthesis. The new position in turn generates its own opposition, and the process continues until all contradictions have been resolved, a state Hegel called the absolute.

This progression as a process in history is a Hegelian innovation. The progression is not something that may happen over an individual life, but is an historical evolution. Karl Marx took the Hegelian dialectic and turned it into dialectical materialism, so that the contradictions and their synthesis are generated by the economic relations of different classes, grounded in technological development. Individuals become vehicles for class struggle. Something analogous is implicated in the Hegelian original, but at the level of concept rather than economics.

This rational progress towards the absolute extends to nature. Philosophical thinking about nature therefore begins with the output of the empirical sciences and from this tries to discover the conceptual structures that are determining the appearance of natural entities and events.

It then turns its attention towards the cultural mind and its productions, becoming the philosophy of *Geist*. The German term *Geist* is usually translated into English as *spirit*, but this doesn't really capture the meaning, which covers the concepts of the mind and cultural acquisition. The term *spirit* also has implications of immateriality, and this can set up a false dichotomy.

The first target of this philosophical project is subjective *Geist*. Subjective *Geist* is divided into two disciplines. The anthropological discipline is concerned with the soul and the capacity for sensation and perception, while the psychological discipline is concerned with the capacity for reason. There is a familiar progression from sensation of individuated entities and events to perception, which is the recognition of these singularities as instances of general concepts, and then to the level of understanding demonstrated in the sciences, where perceived entities and events are understood to be the products of underlying forces.

The second target of the project is objective *Geist*. Objective *Geist* is the set of culturally determined institutions and practices that are recognised by the members of a society. Subjective *Geist* depends on objective *Geist* and this introduces the second significant innovation in Hegel's thinking, the role of other minds in the generation of self-awareness. Kant had suggested that self-awareness, the distinction between self and not-self, is grounded in awareness of the difference between necessary and contingent relations. Hegel argued that the ability to distinguish the self from the not-self was dependent on intersubjective recognition. This idea is illustrated by the master–servant dialectic, where each recognises themselves in the mirror of the other. It is in this process of mutual recognition that objective cultural products such as religious practices and law are generated.

Objective *Geist* is initially internalised and taken as given but, through the process of rational reflection, later comes to be viewed critically, and it is this movement which signals the possibility of the transition to absolute *Geist*. There is an intuitive logic to this. If rational coherence is a constraint on the evolution of conceptual thinking, it seems reasonable to suppose that it can and does progress through the continuous elimination of internal and external incoherence and inconsistency. However, this dynamic doesn't take into account that there are also processes of discovery and innovation, and episodes of wholesale re-orientation of conceptual thinking. More fundamentally, it doesn't take into account the possibility of an intransigent plurality and incommensurability.

Working from the same Kantian inheritance, Hegel's rival Arthur Schopenhauer came to quite different conclusions. Schopenhauer's doctoral dissertation of 1813 was called *The Fourfold Root of the Principle of Sufficient Reason*. Schopenhauer argued that the basis of the principle was the distinction between subject and object, as sufficient explanation was something that a cognitive subject would want to bring to an entity or event as the objective target of cognition. Sufficient explanation meant giving an account of why a state of affairs was necessary. There are four types of necessary connection: cause and effect, which applies to material entities; logical inference, which applies to concepts; quantification, which applies to mathematics; and moral reasoning, which applies to actions and intentions. These connections can't be mixed but apply to different conceptions, an argument that was the basis of his rejection of the arguments of Hegel.

Schopenhauer's principal work is *The World as Will and Representation*. These are the two modes in which the world is apprehended. Representations are what are perceived externally and objectively; will is what is perceived internally and subjectively. The target in both cases is the same. We can understand this in the case of our own bodies, where we apprehend both the intention to do something and the action of doing it, both the internal and the external, but Schopenhauer argues that it applies to everything, including what would usually be considered inanimate entities. The world as a totality therefore has this double-sidedness. The world as representation is how the world appears to cognitive subjects while the world as will is how it is in reality.

Schopenhauer characterises this will as singular and without meaning or purpose. The world as it is represented is an objectification created by the mind. This objectification has a two-level structure. The first level corresponds to the Platonic forms which exist outside space and time. There is therefore an idea of the tree and an idea of the horse, but not multiple instantiations of these as individuated trees and horses. The second level corresponds to the world of experience, where there are individuated entities and events which exist in space and time and are tied together by causal connections. The driver for this layering is the principle of sufficient reason. Where Kant had argued that individuation was the product of the intuitions of space and time and twelve logical categories of judgement, Schopenhauer identified the principle of sufficient reason as the ground of individuation, as the entry on Schopenhauer in the *Stanford Encyclopedia of Philosophy* elaborates:

> *In The World as Will and Representation, Schopenhauer often refers to an aspect of the principle of sufficient reason as the principle of individuation (principium individuationis), linking the idea of individuation explicitly with space and time, but also implicitly with rationality, necessity, systematicity and determinism. He uses the principle of sufficient reason and the principle of individuation as shorthand expressions for what Kant had more complexly referred to as space, time and the twelve categories of the understanding (viz., unity, plurality, totality, reality, negation, limitation, substance, causality, reciprocity, possibility, actuality [Dasein], and necessity).*

What happens when this principle of individuation is imposed on the restless, meaningless and purposeless striving of the will? Almost certainly strife, frustration, violence and suffering, and it is with this pessimism that Schopenhauer imagines the world.

It's easy to overstate the level of scientific progress that had been made in the course of the 17th and 18th centuries. Although the science of mechanics was well-established, chemistry, biology and the Earth sciences were still at a formative stage at the beginning of the 19th century. However, this was a period of significant progress, and by around 1870 there would be, in addition to a well-worked theory of classical mechanics, a theory of electromagnetism connecting electric current, magnetism and light; the organisation of the elements into the periodic table; the development of cell theory and the theory of evolution; and an understanding of the basic principles of geology, though the age of the Earth was still being significantly underestimated. By the middle of the 19th century the rapid development of the natural sciences meant that the Hegelian style of speculative metaphysics was becoming increasingly implausible. The progress made in the natural sciences in the 19th century was kinder to Schopenhauer than to Hegel and, while Hegel's influence waned, Schopenhauer gained increasing recognition in his later life.

A significant component of the institutional form of that development was the establishment of a new kind of university. The model was the University of Berlin which had been founded in 1810 as part of an extensive reform of the Prussian state. This reform process followed Prussia's defeat in 1806, at the battle of Jena, during the Napoleonic wars. Inspired by the ideas of Wilhelm von Humboldt, the new university was intended to be both a teaching and a research institution, and was founded on the notion that the purpose of education was the development of the rounded self-directed individual. The university was to be guided by the principles of disciplinary autonomy and academic freedom, that is, freedom from the constraints of doctrine and utility imposed by church and state respectively.

The new universities formed the apex of the Prussian system of education, which now imposed compulsory schooling. Modernisation was slower in Britain, where the University of London was founded in 1838 under the influence of utilitarian reformers such as Jeremy Bentham, and France, where the system of specialist and elitist *grandes écoles* was being augmented in parallel to the traditional universities. Laboratories, which were previously largely private and amateur institutions, now became part of the university. University education was still restricted to male students; it was only towards the end of the 19th century that women would be admitted and the institutional barriers to women's participation would start to disappear.

Both magnetism and electricity have been known since antiquity, magnetism in the form of naturally occurring lodestones, electricity as a natural phenomenon that could be obtained by rubbing amber. The term electricity comes from the Greek word for amber. An English physician, William Gilbert, published the first systematic treatise on the topic in 1600, and while there was much progress in understanding both over the next two centuries, it wasn't until 1819 that Hans Christian Ørsted made the connection between the two phenomena.

The first electric motor was invented by Michael Faraday in 1821, and it was Faraday, through his work on magnetism, who introduced the concept of a field. The theoretical unification of electricity and magnetism and the identification of light as an electromagnetic phenomenon was completed by James Clark Maxwell. In a paper called *A dynamical theory of the electromagnetic field* published in 1864, Maxell was able to conclude that light was an electromagnetic disturbance that propagated through an electromagnetic field. The concept of the electron as the unit of electromagnetic charge, and the idea that electricity was the movement of electric charge in a wire, was first posited in 1874 by George Johnstone Stoney.

The modern idea of a material substance is based on the concept of an interchangeable stuff. The idea of a chemical substance was first proposed by Joseph Proust in 1794. According to this idea, being a substance implies having a constant composition, which means that any sample of a substance will have the same composition as any other sample. The modern idea of a substance is therefore almost the opposite of the Aristotelian idea; the original idea was that a substance is a singular individuated entity such as a tree, a horse or a bridge; the modern idea is that a substance is a sample of some stuff such as water or carbon that is interchangeable with any other sample of the same stuff.

Chemistry as a scientific discipline was only slowly disentangled from the practice of alchemy. Robert Boyle's book *The Sceptical Chymist* appeared in 1661 and is considered to be one of the first attempts to create an organised theory of how things clump together.

During the 18th century the principal controversy in chemistry was concerned with the nature of combustion, and the postulated role of a substance called phlogiston, which was thought to be burnt in combustion. Antoine Lavoisier was one of the leading figures responsible for identifying that it was oxygen that was the basis of combustion and disproving the existence of phlogiston. Lavoisier was also responsible for bringing precision to chemical experiments and order to the nomenclature of chemical compounds. His major work, *Elementary Treatise on Chemistry*, was published in 1786.

Some 27 separate elements and around 55 compound substances were known to Lavoisier. In the early 18th century John Dalton realised that the weights of the elements were straightforward multiples of the weight of hydrogen, a discovery that indicated that it might be possible to put the elements into some sort of order. In the periodic table that Dimitri Mendeleev presented to the Russian Chemical Society in 1869 there were 56 elements. As proof of the approach, Mendeleev was able to predict from gaps in the table the existence of the then unknown elements germanium, gallium and scandium. By the end of the century, 80 of the 94 elements known to occur naturally had been discovered; a further 24 have subsequently been synthesised.

Where chemistry evolved from the practice of alchemy, biology evolved from the practice of medicine. The inherited knowledge of anatomy in Europe was derived from the work of the Greek physician Galen in the 2nd century, again mediated and augmented trough the Arab world, most influentially in the work of Ibn Sina, known in Europe as Avicenna. Botany centred on the medicinal use of plants and the cultivation of physic gardens for herbalism.

The year 1543 was something of an *annus mirabilis* for new learning. As well as Copernicus' heliocentric cosmology, it was also the year in which, in Padua, Andreas Vesalius published the work *On the Fabric of the Human Body,* which would begin to free anatomy from dependence on ancient authorities and set it on a more scientific path. Influenced by Vesalius's school, William Harvey, who studied in Padua, achieved the most significant early breakthrough, establishing in 1628 the circulation of blood and the role of the heart as a pump.

The microscope was invented at much the same time and place as the telescope. Robert Hooke in his book *Micrographia*, published in 1664, was the first to apply the term *cell* to self-contained units of living matter, in his description of cork tissue. In 1674, Anton van Leeuwenhoek, using superior microscopes, was able to detect microscopic single celled plants and animals in samples of water. Leeuwenhoek's microscopes were made from small fragments of glass ground into near spheres and placed in small metal holders. He was the first to observe sperm cells and postulated that the cell contained a microscopic human being that grew in the womb.

The biological sciences were still largely natural history, focusing on observation, collection, and categorisation rather than theory construction or experiment. The major achievement in the 18th century had been taxonomic, the development of the system of binomial classification by Carl Linnaeus, which was built on morphological resemblances. Linnaeus, who was professor of anatomy and botany at the university of Uppsala in Sweden, published his *Systema Naturae* in 1735. At this time, it was still tenable to interpret the commonality of form of amphibians, reptiles, birds and mammals in Platonic terms as the consequence of the unity of an archetype manifesting itself in different forms according to practical requirements.

The three significant components of the modern biological sciences are cell theory, the evolution of species, and the mechanism of genetic inheritance. Plants cells are significantly larger and easier to see than animal cells. The discovery of the cell nucleus was made by Robert Brown in 1831, based on his observations of plants at Kew Gardens. The insight that all living organisms are composed of cells came through the collaboration of Matthias Schleiden and Theodor Schwann. Schleiden studied plant cells, Schwann animal cells. Schleiden's *Contributions to our Knowledge of Phytogenesis* was published in 1838 and demonstrated that plants are composed of cells. Schwann extended the idea to animals. In his book, *Microscopic Investigations on the Similarity of Structure and Growth of Animals and Plants*, published in 1839, he articulated the idea that all living things are composed of cells and cell products.

This established two of the three basic tenets of cell theory: that all living organisms are composed of one or more cells and that the cell is the basic unit of life. The process of cell division was first described by Robert Remak, leading to the articulation of the third basic tenet, that all cells come from cells – *omnia cellula e cellula* – which was popularised by Rudolf Virchow, in 1855. Virchow borrowed the phrase, and seems also to have borrowed Remak's research, which he published as his own. The story is told in a BBC programme *The Cell: the hidden kingdom.*

At roughly the same time, the theory of evolution of species by natural selection was being developed by Alfred Russel Wallace and Charles Darwin. In 1809 Jean-Baptiste Lamarck had published the first theory of evolution. However, Lamarck's theory depended on the possibility of spontaneous generation and, in the interim, the principle that all cells come from cells had made the idea of spontaneous generation obsolete. Darwin published *On the Origin of Species* in 1859. If cells come from cells, the theory of evolution demonstrated that species come from species, that is, the population of living organisms that exists at a later time has evolved from the population of living organisms that existed at an earlier time.

Although organisms reproduce themselves, so that traits and characteristics are inherited, they reproduce themselves with variations. Because there is competition for resources, and not every organism can reproduce, and because some variations confer a reproductive advantage, the consequence is that there will be an evolution of structure and behaviour in the population of living organisms.

The third component of the synthesis, the idea of the gene and the genetic basis of inheritance, was proposed by Gregor Mendel in 1866, based on his experiments with pea plants. However, the value of this work was not recognised until 1900, when this work was rediscovered, independently, by Hugo de Vries and Carl Correns. The DNA molecule was first identified in 1869 but its double helix structure and its role in genetics would not be understood until the middle of the 20th century.

The concept of evolution of species became part of the debate over the age of the Earth. This was wrapped into a debate about whether terrestrial change was gradual, a view called *uniformitarianism*, or sudden, a view called *catastrophism*. James Hutton's *Theory of the Earth*, first published in 1788, argued that there was uniformity to natural processes through time, and that the Earth was formed gradually by processes that were continuous and continuing. Hutton's principle of uniformity informed Charles Lyell's *Principles of Geology* which in turn informed Darwin's *On the Origin of Species*.

While substantial progress was being made in the natural sciences during this period, there had not yet been a systematic attempt to apply the scientific method to human societies, cultures and cultural artefacts. The social sciences began to take shape during the 1860's, and this in turn would raise questions about the applicability of the scientific method to human cultures and human artefacts. Were there unchanging laws that governed the evolution of human societies, or were they historical developments. In turn this would raise questions about the scientific method: was it a unchanging method with universal applicability, or was science itself an historical product, and what did this mean for the validity of the natural sciences.

6. Nature, culture and history

While the disciplines of biology, chemistry and geology began to take their modern shape in the first half of the 19th century, it was only in the second half of the century that there was also the systematic application of the scientific approach to the human mind and its cultural products, leading to the emergence of the social sciences and the university disciplines of psychology, economics and sociology, along with political science, linguistics, anthropology and comparative religion.

The pioneer in the development of psychology was Gustav Fechner, who initiated the field of psychophysics. Fechner worked in Leipzig. Psychophysics attempted to establish a quantitative correlation between the psychological experience of an event and the underlying physics of the same event. His major work, *Elements of Psychophysics*, was published in 1860. At roughly the same time, also in Leipzig, William Wundt set up the first psychology laboratory, at the university there. In Berlin, Herman Ebbinghaus, inspired by Fechner, pioneered the development of quantitative models of memory. His major work *Memory: A Contribution to Experimental Psychology* was published in 1885.

Political economy, as the study of the political significance of economic activity, developed out of 18th century moral philosophy in the work of Adam Smith, David Ricardo and Jean-Baptiste Say. The emergence of the mathematical study of economics is usually attributed to the development of neoclassical economics in the work of William Jevons, whose book *A General Mathematical Theory of*

Political Economy appeared in 1862, and Alfred Marshall, whose *Principles of Economics* was published in 1890.

The first person to propose that the scientific approach could also be applied to human societies and cultural artefacts was Auguste Comte. His *Course of Positive Philosophy*, which appeared in six volumes between 1830 and 1842, first re-iterates the natural sciences as they were known at the time and then examines the possibility of a science of sociology. In Comte's work, sociology is not just the study of society, it is also the culmination of the sciences. Because the sciences themselves are sociological products, Comte's conception of sociology would make it a rival to philosophy as the discipline that is applicable to itself.

However, this was not to be the idea of sociology that prevailed. The pioneers of the modern conception of sociology were Émile Durkheim and Max Weber. Durkheim, in his *Rules of the Sociological Method*, published in 1895, defined sociology as the science of institutions. Weber, whose major work *The Protestant Ethic and the Spirit of Capitalism* appeared in 1905, considered sociology to be an interpretative science concerned with social action – social action being action as it was conceived by the actor.

With all fields of knowledge increasingly being occupied by the sciences, the role of philosophy would be called into question. Was there still a place for metaphysics, and its concern with the principles of existence, which went beyond physics? Was it possible that the scientific approach could be extended to the reflective mind and its products, so that sociology or psychology might replace philosophy as the discipline whose target domain includes itself, as Comte proposed?

Wilhelm Dilthey was among the first theorists to consider the grounding principles of the developing sciences which concerned themselves with the human mind and its cultural products. Dilthey was professor of philosophy at the University of Berlin from 1882 until his death in 1911. He sought to create a critique of historical reason that would complement Kant's critique of pure reason.

During his time in Berlin, Dilthey's thinking evolved through three phases. His first significant work was *Introduction to the Human Studies,* published in 1883. In this book, he distinguished between the *Naturwissenschaften,* the intellectual disciplines concerned with nature, and the *Geisteswissenschaften,* the intellectual disciplines concerned with human beings and human culture, disciplines that included not only the social sciences but also the humanities, history and the creative arts. In this period, Dilthey hoped to uncover the lawlike structures of inner experience.

In the second phase, in essays such as *The Origin of Our Belief in the Reality of the External World and Its Justification*, published in 1890, and *Ideas for a Descriptive and Analytic Psychology,* published in 1894, Dilthey developed the idea of lived experience. Our inner experience of life engages not only with conceptual representations, but also with meaning, values and purposes. For this reason, it is necessary to distinguish understanding as theoretical explanation in the Kantian sense from understanding as a wider process that gathers together all the functions of the mind; not just reasoning, but also feeling, valuing and willing.

The third phase is marked by the publication in 1900 of *The Rise of Hermeneutics* and, in 1910, of his most significant work *The Formation of the Historical World in the Human Sciences*. Here, he argued that the understanding of lived experience can only be achieved through the interpretation of the objectifications of the cultural mind. Hermeneutics interprets cultural products in order to understand the inner life that produced them. Dilthey sought to apply this way of thinking about lived experience to the understanding of history.

A fundamental term in Dilthey's thinking is *Zusammenhang* ('hanging-togetherness'), which carries the idea of interconnectedness, the way that things hang together in patterns and structures, and its many compounds, particular *Wirkungszusammenhang,* where *Wirkung* means *effect* or *action*. *Wirkungszusammenhang* refers to the patterns and structures that flow from the interaction of multiple dynamics originating from multiple sources.

A second set of fundamental terms derive from *Leben,* the term for life. *Erlebnis* means lived experience (in the sense of a state or condition of the self as a consequence of an event undergone), while *Lebenserfahrung* means experience in the sense of knowledge derived from living, and *Lebensbezüge* are objects which have significance in human lives. Self-understanding is gained by understanding the objects that have such significance.

Although Dilthey can be seen to be moving towards a recognition of what Hegel called objective *Geist*, it is only a partial movement which avoids the teleology implicit in Hegel. Individuals are not vessels or vehicles of some larger purpose. The individual is not subsumed in a culture but is both producer and product of many different objectifications, both the source and the effect, which is the core meaning of *Wirkungszusammenhang*. Meaning, value and purpose are products, at the same time, of individuals, cultures, institutions and societies; entities at all scales are both sources and outcomes of such patterns and structures in which there is an interconnectedness of actions and effects.

This also provides a clue to the difference between social science and history, and a nuance that needs to be added to the concept of *Geisteswissenschaften*. Social science, like natural science, deals in classes of object rather than singular objects. It is explanation at a higher level of abstraction. History, on the other hand, like the creative arts, deals in the singular, the individuated entity and event as the locus of interactions of multiple kinds, rather than as the singular instantiation of a type. What this means is that individuals can't be viewed simply as instances of a class, because individuals participate in every interaction as a whole rather than as an abstraction. There is therefore a trade-off to be made in understanding; the fuller the characterisation, the smaller the population to which it can be applied, and the fullest characterisation applies only to the singularity that is an individual.

Another difference between the natural sciences and the social sciences and humanities is the experience of time. Natural time is symmetrical, so the past, present and future are the same. Historical time, on the other hand, is cumulative, so the present contains the past and anticipates the future. This historical idea of time is a condition of meaning, value and purpose, as these have evolved in historical time.

In an essay called *Types of world-views*, published in 1911, Dilthey described the concept of a world-view. This is the traditional translation of the term *Weltanschauung*, though *world-intuition* might be better. A world-view or world-intuition, which may not be explicitly articulated, is a global perspective that at some level unifies theoretical beliefs, courses of action, and values and, for that reason, contains ontological, logical and epistemological assumptions.

Dilthey identified three common metaphysical world-views. The first, naturalism, which is the world-view that aligns itself to science, Dilthey regarded as too reductive. The second type, the idealism of freedom, he associated with Plato and Kant and the ethics of unconditional freedom. The third type, objective idealism, is more Hegelian, and intuits an ultimate harmony to the cosmos.

World-views are typically products of religion and the creative arts as well as philosophy. Dilthey suggested that religious world-views seek to orient life towards the unknowable, considered as what would later be called the numinous rather than the noumenal. Numinous is a term that was introduced by Rudolf Otto in his book *The Idea of the Holy*, published in 1917, and means inspiring emotion through mystical experience.

Dilthey had a significant influence of the principal philosophical movements of the late 19th and early 20th century, without himself belonging to any of them. These movements were neo-Kantianism, phenomenology and logical positivism.

The motivation for neo-Kantianism was both an opposition to the speculative metaphysics of Hegel but at the same time a rejection of view that the theory of knowledge was equivalent to psychology. Psychology might be able to tell you what was believed, and how and why, but couldn't answer the question whether or not it should be believed, the question of justification. To do this, to establish objective knowledge, it was necessary to follow the kind of critical approach that Kant had taken. At the same time, metaphysics shouldn't be trying to discern in nature the actions of speculative entities such as the *Zeitgeist*. It should be trying to understand science, not direct it.

There were two branches to neo-Kantianism, a northern one centred on the university of Marburg, whose leading figures were Hermann Cohen, Paul Natorp and, later, Ernst Cassirer, and a southern one centred around the universities of Heidelberg and Freiburg, which was led by Wilhelm Winkelband and Heinrich Rickert. The Marburg school was concerned particularly with the conditions of scientific knowledge, and their focus of attention was the mathematical sciences. The southern school, in contrast, was more oriented towards the rules that would enable thinking to achieve the condition of objective validity, with greater focus on the new disciplines of the social sciences.

Both branches believed that objective validity is grounded in non-empirical standards rather than being discovered through experience. However, they rejected Kant's conception of a noumenal and therefore unknowable reality, so these standards were neither given in intuitive experience nor imposed by a conceptual structure in the mind. Rather, they are cultural products, and, as such, they have a history, and evolve as cultures evolve. What counts as reliable knowledge changes as methods and disciplines evolve.

The southern branch was primarily focused on the *Geisteswissenschaften*, the study of human societies and cultures that are now the domain of the social sciences and the humanities. In his essay *History and Natural Science*, Windelband, in contrast to Dilthey, saw the methodological difference between the natural and the social sciences as the difference between the scientific search for the general laws whose operation is discernible in natural events and the historical search for an understanding of singular entities and events. In this view, the social sciences such as psychology align with physics as a consequence of their shared methodology, rather than with history and the creative arts, despite sharing the same object domain with these disciplines. Windelband's main target is the positivist philosophy of history, defended by Comte and John Stuart Mill, which argued that history and the sciences had the same aim: the discovery of the general laws that explain and predict all types of events.

In *The Limits of Concept Formation in Natural Science*, Rickert developed this distinction into a logic. While the sciences work through abstraction, history is concerned with forming the concept of an individuated entity. This is not the complete individual concept of Leibniz' thinking, but rather the components of the individual concept that determine some entity or event's historical significance. The historical method is the general method for determining the historically salient attributes of an individuated entity or event.

The Marburg branch, on the other hand, was more preoccupied with contemporary developments in physics, arguing that these demonstrated that the fundamental ontology of physics is not static but evolves through time. Anticipating future thinking in the philosophy of science, Cassirer argued that there was no objective truth against which the success of science could be judged. He anticipated that this would raise the question as to what then created the possibility of objectivity in science, if radically different ontologies were possible. In response, Cassirer argued that, in judging between scientific theories, there were a set of formal considerations such as scope and simplicity that should be applied. Descartes had suggested similar considerations, but more as a holding device before he was ready with a demonstrative argument from first principles.

There were a couple of significant revolutions in the ontology of physics in this period which support this understanding. One concerned the micro-scale of atomic systems, the other the macro-scale of the cosmos.

The first development was the discovery that atoms, despite the name, had internal structure. Experiments with cathode rays led J. J. Thomson to the identification of electrons in 1897. By 1914, a model of the atom as a dense nucleus surrounded by a less dense zone of electrons had been developed. The discovery that the nucleus of an atom also has internal structure followed from experiments carried out by Ernest Rutherford. Rutherford hypothesised that the nucleus contained hydrogen atoms. In 1920 these bound hydrogen atoms were called protons to distinguish them from unbound hydrogen atoms. At first, the nucleus was thought to be composed of protons and neutral electrons or neutrons, but in 1932 James Chadwick demonstrated that neutrons were slightly more massive than protons. It was these discoveries about the structure of the atom led to the development of quantum mechanics.

The second development was a revolution in the understanding space and time. For light to be the wave-like disturbance in a medium proposed by James Clark Maxwell, it was necessary to postulate the existence of a substance called the luminiferous ether which would function as the medium. However, the necessary characteristics of the ether were contradictory; for example, it had to interact with light but with nothing else. In 1887, the Michaelson-Morley experiment, which was designed to determine the speed of light, failed to detect any dragging effect that could be due to the presence of the ether.

In 1905, Albert Einstein showed that the concept of the luminiferous ether was dispensable. In the special theory of relativity, the speed of light is constant irrespective of the motions of the source and of any observer. Like one aircraft viewed from another, light should appear to be moving faster to someone moving in the opposite direction than it should to someone moving in the same direction. However, speed is a just a consequence of time and distance in space. If the measured speed of light was the same for all observers, then perhaps it was time and space that were relative to the observer. Einstein postulated that the reason that the speed of light was observed to be constant is that motion is relative to a variable frame of reference rather than to a fixed background.

Ten years later, in 1915, Einstein extended the theory to include gravitational attraction. In the general theory of relativity, space and time are not a fixed and constant situation in which events happen. Instead, the geometry of space and time is modified by the distribution of mass within that geometry.

After neo-Kantianism, the second significant philosophic movement in this period was phenomenology, which originated with the work of Franz Brentano, who posited the idea of the *intentional inexistence* of the objects of thought. Intentionality, in this context, means that there was something thought was about, an object that was its target. The approach underlying Brentano's *Psychology*, published in 1874, was that the contents of the mind consisted of representations of something that they were about and these objects were contained in the representation. Only mental representations had this attribute. The background to this approach is Brentano's interpretation of Aristotle's *De Anima*, where Aristotle argues that the mind takes on the form but not the matter of the object of attention.

Brentano's pupil Edmund Husserl developed this idea into a science of phenomenology. Phenomenology is intended as an account of the representation of experience rather than an account of the real world. Its purpose is descriptive rather than explanatory. Intuitively, we assume that our experience, including our scientific knowledge, is experience of a real world. This is what Husserl calls the natural attitude. In phenomenology, nothing is assumed about the existence of a real world in which experience is anchored. Phenomenology doesn't have an ontology incompatible with the way that physics was developing and therefore science doesn't pose any particular problem for phenomenology. The question as to the ontological status of the real world is bracketed out of consideration in the method of phenomenological reduction, not because the real world is unknowable, but in order to analyse the structure of whatever is being observed without preconceptions. Husserl's term for such bracketing is *epoché*, understood as a method whereby consciousness is approached on its own terms. The idea is that from this standpoint, it should be possible to objectively consider the natural attitude and, with it, the scientific attitude.

The principal entities in Husserl's ontology are acts of conscious experience. However, the method is not primarily concerned with such acts as individual events and their contents as individual objects, but with the intuition of the essences of these objects. In a second reduction, called the eidetic reduction, variations in the object are imagined in order to establish what is essential to its being of a certain type. The eidetic reduction brackets the contingent in order that the necessary essences show themselves as eidetic intuitions.

For example, what is essential to something that makes it a bridge? In an imaginative exercise, you can vary the dimensions, the type, the material construction, the type of traffic and so on, but since you cannot imagine a bridge that doesn't span a gap, you can conclude that it is this that is essential to being a bridge.

Unlike Kant, Husserl doesn't consider the real world to be noumenal. The content of an act of consciousness can be a real-world object and part of the act of consciousness is an attitude, belief, hope, desire or fear concerning that object. Husserl calls the content of conscious thought the *noema* and the attitude the *noesis*. These attitudes give an act its quality, where the intentional objects give it its matter. Real-world objects are presented in conscious acts, and when the content of consciousness is associated with a real-world object it will be accompanied by sensory inputs, which Husserl calls *hyle*.

Husserl analyses perceptual experiences both synchronically and diachronically. Synchronically, we don't just perceive from a point-of-view. There is both an internal and external horizon. The internal horizon is the object as it would appear from multiple points-of-view. The external horizon is the environment that comes with the object. Diachronically, experiences are not momentary in time, but have extent or duration and exist as a stream rather than as discrete events. An experience is a composite of the just past, the present and the anticipated near future. These form the temporal horizon of experience in the way that multiple perspectives form the spatial horizon. For example, we anticipate what the rear of a building will look like, or we expect it to fall within a range of possibilities, from our perception of the front, and we can verify that by walking around it. This flow of representations, the stream of consciousness, cannot itself be put in parentheses; there is no gap between experience and reality in this case.

This analysis creates the groundwork for an approach to the unity of consciousness through time and therefore a basis for an account of personal identity. Hume had suggested that he could not locate a self that was separate from his stream of experiences and therefore could not provide any answer to the question of the unity of consciousness either synchronically or diachronically. How are a set of experiences the experiences of one person? Kant, in responding to Hume, argues that there is a continuing self that unites experiences into a stream but that this self is noumenal and not itself apprehensible in experience.

Husserl agreed with Kant that there was a unifying self, but argued that it was in some way apprehensible in experience. The idea of the self, as well as the idea of other selves, is constructed intersubjectively. We attribute conscious acts of experience to others because they behave, more or less, like us. This belief is part the background environment, or *umwelt*, that forms the rational structure underlying the natural attitude. The contents of these environments exercise a motivating force on us, they have a meaning. They form the horizon of possibilities for an individual, and, where they are shared by members of a community, the possibilities for that community. In so far as they are shared by human beings generally, they form the horizon of possibilities for humanity. Because we see others as being like ourselves, we see ourselves in others. We recognise our own corporeal and temporal unity because we see corporeal and temporal unity in others. We see ourselves as one among many, and the coincidence of behaviour implies that we must also be sharing the same real objective world.

The third philosophical movement at this time was logical positivism or logical empiricism (the terms can be used interchangeably), which was the empirical philosophy of the Vienna and Berlin circles. The leader of the Vienna circle was Moritz Schlick, who became professor of philosophy at the University of Vienna from 1922, and other important members were Otto Neurath and Rudolf Carnap. The leading figure in the Berlin circle was Hans Reichenbach.

The movement embraced diverse concerns and perspectives but there was a common concern with the scientific method and the role of ontology, epistemology, logic and mathematics in modern science. It was influenced by the contemporary advances in logic made by Gottlob Frege and Bertrand Russell and the early theories of language developed by Ludwig Wittgenstein. There was also a political and cultural dimension to the movement, somewhat analogous in its concerns to the Enlightenment of the 18th century. As Peter Godfrey-Smith puts it in his book *Theory and Reality*:

> *Logical positivism was a plea for Enlightenment values, in opposition to mysticism, romanticism, and nationalism. The positivists championed reason over the obscure, the logical over the intuitive. The logical positivists were also internationalists, and they liked the idea of a universal and precise language that everyone could use to communicate clearly.*

Obscurantism, mysticism, nationalism and romanticism were associated with reactionary politics and metaphysics, understood in a pejorative sense. The scientific approach was seen as necessary to bring social renewal, which was being held back by unthinking acceptance of the authority of the church and state.

Rudolf Carnap (1891–1970) was perhaps the leading theorist of the movement and his work can be taken to illustrate the main positions and developments. Carnap was a formalist with regard to mathematics, meaning that he saw it as a structure of axiomatic statements and rules of inference for determining logical consequences. Carnap regarded a scientific theory as a logical structure that combined such a set of formal axioms and rules of inference with a set of empirical statements that carried the content. The empirical component was divided into observational and theoretical terms. From these it followed that there could be observational and theoretical statements and also a set of correspondence statements which would bring the two together.

This distinction between the observational and the theoretical was central to the movement. Observation and experiment confirm empirical laws which can be arrived at by generalisation. But not everything is observable; some structures can only be inferred, and these form the content of theoretical laws. However, because theoretical laws predict empirical laws which can be tested, theoretical laws can be validated indirectly.

The second pillar of logical empiricism was the clear demarcation between analytic and synthetic statements and a strict mapping of these to *a priori* and *a posteriori* knowledge. However, this intuitively simple idea proved difficult to formulate with any precision, and Carnap developed various ways of interpreting it, moving from a purely formal and syntactic conception to a semantic conception which allowed that statements derived from other statements which defined the meaning of non-logical terms could still be considered analytic.

In this regard, the logical positivists differed from Kant, who argued for mathematics as a case of the synthetic *a priori*, and from later modal ontologies such as that proposed by Saul Kripke, which argued for the possibility of the analytic *a posteriori*. However, the distinction between analytic and synthetic statements reflects a language-centric way of thinking about scientific theories (and theories generally, for that matter) and I will discuss in the next chapter how language-centric approaches have been displaced by heuristic model-centred approaches.

The third pillar of logical empiricism was the verification theory of the meaning of synthetic statements. This stated that if there was no method, even if only in principle, to test a statement, then it had no meaning. This principle also proved difficult to formulate. Initially, Carnap argued that all the terms used should be reducible to observational terms. However, in 1935, he introduced what he called the principle of tolerance, which held that theoretical terms can become meaningful in the context of the theory in which they are deployed. The principle of tolerance is that there is no uniquely correct logic. Alternative positions can be thought of as different possible ways to structure science. These alternatives cannot be evaluated theoretically; they should be regarded as practical proposals. In this formulation, the verification principle has the practical advantage that it eliminates time-wasting on indeterminable arguments, and this is another attribute which distinguishes worthwhile theories, like scope and simplicity.

Carnap's critique of metaphysics was written before he introduced the principle of tolerance into his work. In an essay called *The*

Elimination of Metaphysics Through Logical Analysis of Language, published in 1932, Carnap argued that modern logic had bolstered empirical science and undermined metaphysics. In regard to the former, concepts had been clarified and their connection had been made explicit. In regard to the latter, logical analysis has shown that the statements being made were meaningless:

> But what, then, is left over for philosophy, if all statements whatever that assert something are of an empirical nature and belong to factual science? What remains is not statements, nor a theory, nor a system, but only a method: the method of logical analysis. The foregoing discussion has illustrated the negative application of this method: in that context it serves to eliminate meaningless words, meaningless pseudo-statements. In its positive use it serves to clarify meaningful concepts and propositions, to lay logical foundations for factual science and for mathematics.

The target of Carnap's critique is generally the style of metaphysics practiced by Hegel and, more contemporaneously, Martin Heidegger; and in particular Heidegger's essay *What is Metaphysics?* which had been published in 1929. The problem, Carnap suggests, is twofold. Firstly, there is the confusion of existence statements with classification, identification and attribution statements, due to an ambiguity in most European languages that means that the verb *to be* can mean *is something* and also *exists*. In a logical language, on the other hand, the proper form is *There is an x such that x is an instantiation of type y*, where the first part is the existential statement and the second the classification, attribution or identification.

Descartes' statement *I think, therefore I am* can be shown to rest on a logical error. The full meaning of the first clause can be elaborated as *There is an I such that I think,* and the second clause as *There is an I,* meaning that it is simply restating the premise. The idea is that existence can only be predicated of a predicate, so the full argument would be *There is an I such that I think, therefore there is thinking.*

The second source of confusion is the ambiguity of type. The source of the problem is the flexibility of language, so that the same syntactic and morphological forms are used to describe different types of structure, and this leads philosophers astray. To illustrate his argument, Carnap quotes phrases from Heidegger's essay *What is Metaphysics?* which treats the Nothing, *das Nichts,* as a noun, and to nothing, *nichten,* as a verb:

> Where do we seek the Nothing? How do we find the Nothing... We know the Nothing... Anxiety reveals the Nothing... That for which and because of which we were anxious, was "really" nothing. Indeed: the Nothing itself – as such – was present... What about this Nothing? – The Nothing itself nothings (das Nicht nichts).

Carnap's critique is that while these phrases are syntactically correct, they are semantically empty because the words *das Nichts* and *nichten* don't have any discernible meaning in these phrases.

The point of Carnap's argument can be illustrated with Noam Chomsky's syntactically correct but semantically invalid construct *Colourless green ideas sleep furiously*; it is meaningless because we can sleep soundly but we cannot sleep furiously; sleeping is not a state that ideas can be in; while ideas can be new, they cannot have a colour, green or otherwise, and what is green cannot also be colourless. In the language of data modelling, none of these are valid attributes and values for the type *idea*.

In natural language, creating such types is intuitive. By that I mean that the rules which constrain what attributes and values can be applied to entities and events are not declared explicitly, in the way that data structures are declared at the start of a computer program, or the variables and constants are declared at the start of a piece of mathematical reasoning, or the meaning of terms is stipulated in a legal document – all contexts where ambiguity would be a significant problem. But though they are undeclared in natural language and therefore understood intuitively, the rules are still there.

There are a couple of observations that can be made about Carnap's argument. One is that neither the syntax nor the semantics of a natural language are fixed. They can and will be extended, not just by writers, but in the everyday course of the evolution of speech, in order to find a way of saying something which isn't possible with the language as it is.

Since there will always be new knowledge, there will always be a requirement to develop the language to articulate it, which points to the limitations inherent in the idea that there can be a logically complete and unambiguous language. Chomsky's construct is meaningless because no data model that would give it meaning has yet been developed, but it remains a possibility that one could be. I will consider the meaning of Heidegger's essay in the next section.

The second is that metaphysics is not so easily dispensable. The facile rebuttal of the verification principle is that it doesn't meet its own criterion for meaning, since it is not itself empirically testable. Nevertheless, it clearly is meaningful. There are many other criteria by which metaphysical arguments can be assessed critically; criteria such as simplicity, scope, coherence, consistency, adequacy, necessity and absence of arbitrariness. However, these criteria apply at the scale of disciplines and discourses, rather than judgement by judgement, and therefore don't fit into what Quine was to call the reductivism of the logical positivist's model of language.

By the time Carnap wrote this essay, these three philosophical movements had largely run their course. Neo-Kantianism had been the leading movement in Germany since the middle of the 19th century, but in the spring of 1929, Cassirer had engaged in a colloquy with Heidegger at the *Hochschule* in Davos, on the subject of Kantianism and philosophy, and had come off the worse in the debate, in the view of most observers, including Cassirer himself. I will also discuss this debate further in the next section.

In January 1933, the Nazi party gained a majority in the Reichstag and Adolf Hitler was appointed German chancellor, in addition assuming the presidency the next year. Many scientists, writers, artists and philosophers left Germany to avoid the Nazis' totalitarian *Gleichschaltung* programme. Schlick was murdered by a student. Carnap and Reichenbach and many other members of the Berlin and Vienna circles emigrated to the United States and become influential teachers at American universities. Husserl remained in Germany, but was unable to teach or publish.

Heidegger, who seems to have seen a reflection of his own anti-technology agrarianism in Nazism, accepted the post of rector at Freiburg university in May 1933, in order, he later argued, to defend the German university, before resigning 10 months later.

7. Contemporary world-intuitions

The Aristotelian world-view that dominated European thinking for 500 years was remarkably coherent. The ontology of substances and attributes underpinned the physics of hylomorphism; living organisms were a subset of physical systems capable of growth, sustenance and reproduction; animals were a subset of living organisms that were additionally capable of sensation and perception; and human beings were a subset of animals additionally capable of rational thought. Finally, the subject–predicate structure of rational thought was congruent with the substance-attribute structure of reality, closing the loop.

The coherence of this structure started to come apart in the scientific revolution of the 17th century, which undermined the physics of hylomorphism and with it the other components of the Aristotelian synthesis. The basic challenge for any modern ontology is to find a replacement synthesis that will explain how life, the mind and conceptual rationality relate to physical structures and systems as these are now understood.

Physical, in this context, doesn't imply materiality. The basic notion of a particle in particle physics will be misleading if a particle is taken to be a grain of material. Modern physics is both in theory and experiment a mathematical science. Where a physical structure maps to a mathematical structure the physical structure can be said to satisfy the mathematical structure. Though often treated simply as background, the most fundamental of these mathematical structures are the models of space and time, of which Euclidean space is the most salient, and the extent that they are thought to apply to actual space and time. A particle is a set of physical quantities associated with a location in a model of space and time.

The problem this poses for the wider understanding is illustrated in this explanation of the place of mathematics in physics by Roger Penrose in an interview:

> *I think people often find it puzzling that something abstract like mathematics could really describe reality as we understand it...you think of something like a chair or something you know something made of solid stuff, and then you say...well, what's our best scientific understanding of what that is? Well, you say, it's made of fibres and cells, and so on...and these are made of molecules, and those molecules are made of atoms, those atoms are made out of nuclei and electrons going around, and you say well...what's a nucleus? Then you say...well it's protons and neutrons, and they're held together by things called gluons...and neutrons and protons are made of things called quarks, and so on. And then you say, well what is an electron? And what's a quark? And at that stage, the best you can do is to describe some mathematical structure...you say, they're things that satisfy the Dirac equation, or something like that...which you can't understand what that means, without mathematics.*

There are two transitions in the course of this explanation though they aren't given a particular emphasis. They occur around the scale of atoms and molecules. Firstly, there is the transition from observable to unobservable objects and, secondly, the transition from linguistic structures to mathematical structures, from the logic of subjects and predicates to the logic of conceptual modelling.

It is these transitions that make it hard to explain modern physics using everyday language. In everyday speech we would naturally say *This chair has four legs* rather than *This object satisfies the conceptual structure four-legged chair,* but this familiar syntax is misleading when applied to the ontology of modern physics.

Logical positivism was a linguistic theory of science, and, as such, it became increasingly clear that even in its most sophisticated forms it couldn't be made to work. The sciences just aren't collections of axioms, definitions and logically connected observation and theory statements. The shift from a language-oriented to a model-oriented paradigm has been the most marked development in the philosophy of science over the last few decades. As Peter Godfrey-Smith describes it in his book *Theory and Reality,* which covers developments in the philosophy of science from the logical positivists through to the present:

> The field has become less dominated by questions about language, and proper attention is being paid to model-building as a crucial part of scientific work.

By 1967, John Passmore felt able to declare that logical positivism was as dead as any philosophical movement ever could be. A number of developments had contributed to its demise. In his 1951 paper *Two Dogmas of Empiricism,* W. V. O. Quine challenged two of the core propositions of logical positivism, both the strict distinction between analytic and synthetic statements and the reductive assumption that scientific statements could be confirmed or disconfirmed singly and independently. Quine argued that scientific propositions form a web of belief which has contact with experience only as whole. While acknowledging that this kind of reductivism had long ceased to be a part of Carnap's thinking, he suggested that:

> The dogma of reductionism survives in the supposition that each statement, taken in isolation from its fellows, can admit of confirmation or infirmation at all. My countersuggestion, issuing essentially from Carnap's doctrine of the physical world in the Aufbau, is that our statements about the external world face the tribunal of sense experience not individually but only as a corporate body.

A second change has been the development of two-level models of science and the related recognition of the history and sociology of science. Quine's holism remains, like logical positivism, a single level model of scientific theory, as do rivals such as Karl Popper's model of conjectures and refutations. These theories have been largely displaced by two-level models, of which the most significant is Thomas Kuhn's model of normal and revolutionary science. Kuhn's *The Structure of Scientific Revolutions* was published in 1962. Imre Lakatos also proposed a two-level model, one which focused on competition between research programmes within a shared discipline.

The neo-Kantians had understood that science had a history and evolved through time, an idea that implied that there were extra-scientific criteria being applied to judge between competing theories.

Carnap's principle of tolerance allowed for a pragmatic selection from different linguistic frameworks. In Kuhn's model, normal science is puzzle-solving within the framework of a disciplinary matrix. Normal science is punctuated by periods of revolutionary science in which one disciplinary matrix is replaced by another. The revolution is generated by the accumulation of anomalies. Under normal circumstances, anomalies are tolerated. They are a component of the known unknowns that are the subject of scientific research. However, if the accumulation of anomalies becomes intolerable, it creates a crisis which is resolved in a scientific revolution. The new disciplinary matrix will resolve the anomalies that had accumulated under the displaced paradigm and open fruitful new paths for research.

Kuhn's disciplinary matrix has four components: a set of symbolic generalisations; a commitment to a set of heuristic and ontological models; a set of values; and a set of exemplary past scientific achievements, which Kuhn called *paradigms*, although this term is often loosely applied to the whole of the disciplinary matrix. By its nature, the disciplinary matrix that prevails after a scientific revolution is incommensurable with the disciplinary matrix that prevailed before the revolution; if it were an extension, it wouldn't resolve the anomalies that led to the original crises.

Where Kuhn made the history of science important, later theorists also made the sociology of science important, identifying what Bruno Latour calls the essential politics and polemics of scientific work. String theory is a good example. In his book *The Trouble with Physics*, Lee Smolin discusses the circumstances in which string theory shifted almost overnight from being a marginal interest in particle physics to becoming the dominant research programme, monopolising research funding and career decision-making in a way that squeezed out competing programmes – a development which, in Smolin's view, has contributed to the creation a crisis in the discipline.

A disciplinary matrix defines an intellectual discipline. We could add further elements to Kuhn's list. As well as the generalisations, models, values and exemplary achievements, there are also governance structures, research programmes and traditions, textbooks and teaching, career structures, funding models, journals, conferences and channels of public communication.

With the development of modern physics, the demise of logical positivism, and a new emphasis on history and sociology in the philosophy of science, a new way of thinking about the relationship between structures at different scales and different types was required. The concept of supervenience provides the basic modern framework. This concept was introduced by Donald Davidson in an essay called *Mental Events*, published in 1970:

> *Although the position I describe denies there are psychophysical laws, it is consistent with the view that mental characteristics are in some sense dependent, or supervenient, on physical characteristics. Such supervenience might be taken to mean that there cannot be two events alike in all physical respects but differing in some mental respect, or that an object cannot alter in some mental respect without altering in some physical*

respect. Dependence or supervenience of this kind does not entail reducibility through law or definition: if it did, we could reduce moral properties to descriptive, and this there is good reason to believe cannot be done; and we might be able to reduce truth in a formal system to syntactical properties, and this we know cannot in general be done.

Supervenience is a compositional relation between two structures at different scales or of different kinds. To say that one structure supervenes on another structure means that any modification in the supervening structure must be accompanied by a modification in the structure supervened upon. However, the relationship is asymmetrical, so that a change in the supervened-on structure doesn't necessarily imply a change in the supervening structure.

Although introduced in the context of the problem of mental events and physical events, the supervenience relationship has more general application. For example, it can apply also to relationship between living organisms and physical structures. The supervenience model applies straightforwardly to the problem of the relationship between physics, biology and culture. Biological structures and events supervene on chemical and physical structures and events; cultural structures and events supervene on biological, chemical and physical structures and events.

The philosophical movement called naturalism holds that everything supervenes on the physical, where what is physical is the ontology of the natural sciences. This ontology used to be called scientific materialism; however, the term physicalism is often used, recognising that the ontology of modern physics contains very little materiality. It is this combination of scientific materialism and the view that the scientific method is the only basis of truly reliable knowledge that is distinctive of naturalism as a philosophical movement.

Naturalism is an anti-foundationalist approach to the philosophy of science. Instead of trying to establish from the outside, in the manner of the logical positivists, what valid scientific knowledge looks like, philosophical naturalism builds upon the practice of science, taking scientific and philosophical thinking to be continuous.

Although naturalism as an world-view is older, the origins of modern philosophical naturalism can be found in the work of American pragmatists such as John Dewey and Wilfred Sellars. Quine's paper *Epistemology Naturalised*, published in 1969, is sometimes taken to be the initial formulation. Quine argued that epistemology should be a part of psychology rather than a separate discipline, so that belief formation and change could become the subject of scientific study.

Supervenience is a fairly baggy idea that can be deployed in different ways. As Davidson describes it, it doesn't imply either a methodological or ontological reductivism; however, at the same time, although Davidson thought them implausible, it doesn't rule them out. Reductive methodologies argue that explanations should be reductive, so that culture is explained by psychology, psychology by biology, biology by chemistry and chemistry by physics. Similarly, ontological reductivism is the view that the dynamics driving the evolution of every system function at the micro-scale, so cultural change is driven by psychological change, psychological change by biological change, biological change by chemical change and chemical change by physical change.

In this way of thinking, higher-level explanations are what Daniel Dennett calls *stances*: sets of simplifying assumption that allow us to process complexity, but which should not be taken literally. The theoretical basis of reductive naturalism is the causal closure of physics, the idea that the evolution of every system can be explained by physics, if only in principle. Though not always declared, it is the assumption of the causal closure of physics that lies behind theories of scientific determinism and related debates concerning freedom of the will.

Methodological and ontological reductivism usually go together, as ontological reductivism implies methodological reductivism. However, it is possible to approach problems reductively from a pragmatic perspective, rather than from any ontological commitment, on the basis that the analytic method has proved fruitful in the past.

In practice, because the gap between human experience and physics is too large, reductivism tends to manifest itself as reductionism. The distinction is drawn by Thomas Nagel in his book *Mind and Cosmos*. Reductive theories seek to explain complex wholes in terms of their simplest and most primitive components, while reductionist theories seek to explain rational, cultural and social events as physical, chemical and biological events. Reductionism is the attempt to explain cultural and conceptual entities and events in terms of natural entities and events. Explaining biology and psychology in terms of physics and chemistry is reductive;

explaining the cultural mind and its products in terms of biology and psychology is reductionist. Generally speaking, reductionists will tend to be reductivists, because it would be intuitively odd to accept the autonomy of biology and psychology from physics and chemistry and at the same time deny the autonomy of culture and society from biology and psychology. However, a reductivist doesn't have to be a reductionist. A reductivist could take the view that both psychology and biology are grounded in physics, without supposing that psychological systems align with and are explained by biological structures. Such an approach would lead to the elimination of macro-scale objects as the target of explanation, a position called, not surprisingly, eliminativism.

Although an empirical philosophy, modern philosophical naturalism tends to support scientific realism, the idea that science provides a genuine description and explanation of the real-world-out-there, in some fashion. This may seem obvious but it is a point of view at odds with the empiricist tradition. For most of the 19th century, the empirical tradition – of which John Stuart Mill was the leading representative – had largely adhered to a perspective called *phenomenalism*. This is the idea that all that we have access to are sense experiences and the goal of science was therefore to make sense of these experiences, not to speculate about the nature of the unobservable entities and events that might exist beyond the horizon of sense experience. Logical positivism continued this tradition. The target of observation statements was what could be experienced by the senses, and the target of theoretical statements were unobservable entities and events that could be inferred from a set of observations.

Naturalism can be difficult to pin down, since the label is claimed for many different arguments. Two different types are usually recognised: methodological naturalism and metaphysical naturalism. As a world-view, it is often characterised more by what it excludes than adherence to any particular theory or doctrine. The collection of ideas that are gathered together under the rubric of scientific materialism, scientific realism and scientific determinism are arguably too dogmatic to be properly naturalistic. However, what might be called a reasonable naturalism, that, while recognising the successes of the natural sciences also acknowledges their limitations, wouldn't seem to justify the label, as it would be indistinguishable from a reasonable pluralism.

The restriction that naturalism places on supervenience is that only the nature of reality recognised by science, and those things that supervene on this nature of reality, are recognised. This means that it excludes not only the supernatural and the magical. It also excludes most forms of religious belief. Theism, the view that there is a creator God separate from nature, and panentheism, the view that nature is in God, but God is more than nature, are excluded by the ontology; natural religion, pantheism, and mysticism are excluded by the methodology.

Through its commitment to the scientific method, naturalism also tends to exclude intuition, personal experience and the testimony of others as a basis for knowledge unless also supported scientifically. In contrast, one philosophical movement that is self-consciously reliant on intuitions has been the modern revival of essentialism within analytic philosophy, in which Saul Kripke has been particularly influential. (Kripke's lectures later published as *Naming & Necessity* were also originally delivered in 1970.) This movement posits the existence of natural kinds as the basic reality and the units of analysis for science. Natural kinds are the entities and events of familiar experience: tigers, heat, gold, water and so on. According to this view, the goal of science is to find better descriptions for the familiar and intuitive notions.

Natural kinds serve as the organising principle of nature in a way that is similar to the role of substantive form in hylomorphism but without the teleological dynamic. As Kripke puts it in *Naming & Necessity*:

> In general, science attempts, by investigating basic structural traits, to find the nature, and thus the essence (in the philosophical sense), of the kind.

This is almost certainly not what modern science is doing. Rather, this idea of what science is traying to do comes out of developments in modal logic in the mid-20th century. Modal logic is concerned with statements that contain a modal qualifier: not statements such as *Some x is y*, but statements such as *Some x is necessarily y* or *Some x is contingently y*. In the modal logic of necessity and contingency that was developed at this time, these concepts are described in terms of possible worlds. Some predication is necessary if it is true in all possible worlds, possible if it is true in at least one possible world, and impossible if it is untrue in every possible world. What is possible but not necessary is contingent.

Modal logic is then used as the basis for a new formulation of essentialism. A chair may have four-legs in the actual world but it might have had three legs in some other possible world. However, there is no possible world in which, if it exists at all, it isn't a chair, and so what makes it a chair, its essence, makes it a chair necessarily.

Kripke's analysis in *Naming and Necessity* starts with singular entities, things that have names. So, for instance, William Shakespeare must be the same person in every possible world in which he exists at all, because if he isn't there wouldn't be any justification for applying the name *William Shakespeare*.

This argument is then extended to natural kinds. Since water must have the same molecular composition in every possible world, in any world where it exists a sample of water will be a sample of H_2O molecules. A sample of water is a natural kind and being identical to a sample of H_2O molecules is the essence of the natural kind that has been discovered by science. This implies the possibility of the analytic *a posteriori*. *Water is H_2O* is an analytic statement, but the fact that it is had to be discovered through experience, it could not be arrived at by demonstrative reasoning from first principles.

This is where an appeal to intuition is made. Could a sample of water be anything other than a sample of H_2O, could Shakespeare be anyone else but Shakespeare. These propositions must be necessarily true, mustn't they? The problem with this way of thinking can be illustrated by thinking about the concept of a person. The idea of a person is tied to the idea of a human life as a biological continuity which starts with conception and ends at death. Persons can't switch lives and lives can't split or join. A person is a historical singularity because a human life is a biological singularity.

People are tagged with a label, a name, usually at birth, and may acquire other labels during their lifetime. Those labels identify both the human being and the conceptual structure which accumulates and organises the information about that person's life. The events of someone's life, which are continuously recorded in the structure and build into what might be called the complete individual concept of the person, are contingent – they might have been different – but the continuity and singularity of a human life, once it is begun, is inescapable.

If a human life is a singular historical event, what does it mean to say, for example, that Shakespeare might never have existed or that Shakespeare's life might have turned out differently? The important distinction to make is to be clear whether you mean Shakespeare as the reference to a human life or *Shakespeare* as the name of a conceptual structure. It quite possible that Shakespeare the human being never existed, but that *Shakespeare* the conceptual structure remains the same. Imagine, for instance, that the human life we know had never happened, but another human life had been lived, only delayed by one month. That human being would be a different human being from the one that actually existed, but the difference of one month could be everything or nothing with regard to the concept. It might mean some decisive event never happened, and *William Shakespeare,* the conceptual structure in this alternative scenario, would then have quite different values – the attribute *occupation* being, perhaps, *merchant* rather than *playwright*. On the other hand, the delay of a month could turn out to be immaterial, and the concept *William Shakespeare* that we have could apply equally both to the life that happened and to the life that didn't.

It isn't surprising that pre-scientific classification systems quite often align with scientific taxonomies, but at the same time, they also often don't. It turns out that the traditional elements earth, fire and breathable air don't map conveniently to a chemical element or compound, so, while we identify water as H_2O, we don't identify earth, fire and air in this way. Similarly, because it turns out that whales are mammals rather than fish, the everyday meaning of the term *whale*, which used to refer to any large marine creature, has been adjusted to align to the biological taxonomy.

The modern understanding of biological types is based on genetic inheritance rather than morphology or behaviour and the taxonomy has been adapted to reflect this. Could water be something other than H_2O or gold not have atomic number 79? Not really. Our understanding of material substances is based on our knowledge of physics and chemistry, so that when an everyday classification maps to a chemical element or molecule, we align the two. These identities are not analytic statements, they are bridging statements between two different domains of discourse.

The concepts of modal logic have been used by Alvin Plantinga to put forward a new version of the ontological argument for the existence of God. The argument is that if there is a possible world in which God, defined as a being of maximal greatness, could exist, then that being must exist is every possible world, including the actual world, because existing in every possible world is a feature of maximal greatness. It follows that God exists, because the actual world is one of these possible worlds. The argument is similar to Anselm's original ontological argument with the difference that instead of existence being a component of completeness, existence is an component of maximal greatness.

The argument hangs on a theorem of modal logic to the effect that if something necessary is possible then it is necessary *tout court*. Put in terms of possible worlds, if something is necessary in some world, it also exists in every possible world, including this one, because necessity implies existing in all possible worlds. From this it follows that if God, conceived as a maximally great and therefore necessary being, is possible in any possible world, then God necessarily exists in all possible worlds.

There are any number of objections to this argument. The most basic is that existential necessity and possibility are being argued from logical necessity and possibility, so that a logically possible world, one that can be imagined without contradiction, must also be an ontologically possible world. Even if we were to concede for the sake of argument that existence is a logically necessary attribute of maximal greatness, it doesn't follow that such a being must necessarily exist ontologically; only things that actually exist are possible candidates for maximal greatness.

Plantinga doesn't claim that his argument works as a proof; his purpose is to argue that it is possible for a person to rationally hold a belief in the existence of a God whose nature corresponds to the

Christian conception. The idea is that belief based on direct religious experience or acceptance of the testimony of others regarding such experience can be supplemented by rational argument. Leaving the logic aside, it might be argued that the appeal to faith is not there to supplement the shortcomings of reason, but because only what is held as a matter of faith is held in the right way for religious understanding.

Since the second world war, the centre of gravity of thinking about ontology has been the United States. The most significant movements in Europe – existentialism, Marxism, structuralism, critical theory and post-modernism – have tended to be concerned with the nature of discourse and public reasoning and social, cultural and political critique.

One exception has been Heidegger's continuing influence. In the 20th century, Heidegger is probably the most significant philosopher to posit an ontology which conflicts with the one proposed by the natural sciences. Heidegger's concept of science, articulated in his essay *The Question Concerning Technology*, might be considered a modern version of cardinal Bellarmine's argument against Galileo: the calculations of the mathematical sciences work correctly, but they function to save the appearances, and shouldn't be interpreted as describing the truth of things.

At the Davos *Hochschule* held in March 1929 the principal event was a debate between Cassirer and Heidegger. During the debate Cassirer argued that it was possible through reasoning to move beyond things as they appear to things as they are intelligible, and thereby to transcend the limitations of concrete human experience and gain access to a standpoint that permitted universally applicable truth. This exemplified the world-view that Wilhelm Dilthey had called the idealism of reason.

Heidegger regarded this approach as an evasion which avoided the question of the nature of existence, for which Heidegger used the everyday term for actuality, *Dasein,* taking it very literally to mean *being here.* Heidegger argued that it wasn't possible to transcend concrete experience because existence is bound to the historical and contingent experience of being of a particular human life. This is the basis of his hermeneutical phenomenology. Heidegger argued that philosophy as conceived by Cassirer took as its domain of application the mathematical sciences rather than being concerned with being and existence directly.

Heidegger's thinking developed through his career. The interpretation that follows is based on the essays published after 1929, rather than his major work, *Being and Time,* which was published relatively early in his career, in 1927. The main sources are *What is Metaphysics?* (1929), *The Letter on Humanism* (1947), *Being, Dwelling, Thinking* (1951), *The Question Concerning Technology* (1954) and the posthumously published interview with *Der Spiegel, Only a God can Save Us* (1966).

Heidegger's central question is usually translated as *What is the being of beings?* The terms that are being translated as *being* and *beings* are *das Sein* and *das Seiende. Das Seiende* is composed of the everyday and familiar things that fill the world: landscapes and rivers, plants and animals, buildings, tools and equipment and artworks. *Das Seiende* is the population of things. It is composed of everything that is discernible as a thing, and to be intelligible at all means to be a thing. *Das Seiende* is the total population of discernible entities, or perhaps more accurately, the population of historical events that happen to the population of things.

There is second domain in this ontology, which is *das Nichts*, the nothing. *Das Nichts* is – well actually we can't finish that sentence, because to say *is* is to necessarily speak of *das Seiende*. *Das Nichts* is usually translated as *the nothing* but it is something not nothing, it is better thought of as *the no-thing*, the state where there are no things. The familiar and everyday is concealed in *das Nichts* and unconcealed in *das Seiende*. It is the shelter, the harbour, where the familiar and everyday is concealed and protected; outside time and history, somewhat like the domain of ideas in Plato, though in this case the contents of *das Nichts* are not objects as such, but the building blocks of objects.

This distinction between beings and the nothing is also similar to Kant's distinction between the phenomenal and the noumenal. The two go together like the two sides of a piece of paper. However, while Kant regarded the noumenal as inaccessible to human experience, Heidegger argued that in moments of dread, boredom or joy, it was possible to apprehend *das Nichts* directly.

Everything has a *Wesen*. It is its *Wesen* that determines the way in which something transitions between the concealment of *das Nichts* and the unconcealment of *das Seiende*. The *Wesen* of a bridge is different from the *Wesen* of a tree, so bridges appear to us as bridges and trees appear to us as trees. The transition between *das Nichts* and *das Seiende* Heidegger calls *Anwesen,* which is usually translated as coming-to-presence. *Wesen* means nature or essence. It refers to that which holds sway over how something comes to be intelligible to us.

This transition is not a movement in space. An analogy that suggests itself to me is a Polaroid. The picture is taken and the photograph printed. At first, we see nothing, just a black square, but as we watch the image comes into view. The image was always there but it took a moment for the photograph to develop and the image to become visible. The transition between *das Nichts* and *das Seiende*, between concealment and un-concealment, is analogous to the development of the image.

The *Wesen* specific to human beings is *Dasein*, which can be translated as *existence*. Things can become intelligible only to *Dasein*, and for this reason only *Dasein* exists in Heidegger's model. *Dasein* dwells among and is normally occupied with particular things. Only in certain moods, such as boredom or joy, does *Dasein* apprehend *das Seiende* as a whole, and only in brief moments of dread, when the world of things seems to be slipping away, does *Dasein* have an apprehension of *das Nichts*.

Existence is not, for Heidegger, consciousness, life, culture or mind; it is more a structure that is imposed on a human life. A person, a someone, is a structure thrown onto a human life, the life which is their being. From this, Heidegger argued that there can be no truth outside existence. Without existence, and existence is necessarily a concrete human existence, there is no truth. This doesn't mean that truth is a construct of the human mind or human culture and society. The dependence is one of carrier or conduit, in the way that the existence of a viaduct may be necessary to transport water to the city, but doesn't determine the character of the water.

So the fundamental question isn't why anything should exist but why anything should be intelligible. Existence is inscrutable, but we can ask about intelligibility. I think this is the key to understanding Heidegger's writing. There isn't nothing, so there must be something, but it is confusingly called *das Nichts*. In this ocean of the unknowable there is an island of intelligibility, called *das Seiende*, where things - objects, beings - become discernible.

Things, objects and beings are the same entities. Heidegger changes the terminology to suit the word games he wants to play. In the metaphysical essays the focus is on beings because of the potential for wordplay between *das Sein* and *das Seiende*. In the essay *Building, Dwelling, Thinking* the focus is on things because Heidegger wants to draw on the etymological roots of the word for thing, *Ding*, as the name for a gathering or assembly. In *The Question Concerning Technology* the focus is on objects because of the potential for wordplay between *Bestand*, usually translated as standing-reserve, meaning a fungible stock or supply or store, and *Gegenstand,* a discrete intelligible object.

The key term is *bergen* meaning to hide. Concealing is *verbergen,* the effect of the prefix to intensify the meaning of the idea contained in the stem, and un-concealing is *entbergen*, the effect of the prefix this time is the negation of the idea contained in the stem. The English word *harbour* is the precise equivalent. Harbouring contains both the idea of hiding and also of protecting. Ships take refuge in harbour for protection and fugitives are harboured, that is protectively concealed, from their pursuers. The word *harbour* is derived from an old English term *herebeorg* and therefore has the same etymological roots as *bergen,* as does the French term héberger, meaning to harbour and to shelter.

What then does Heidegger mean by *das Sein*. George Steiner suggested an affinity between Heidegger and the poet Gerard Manly Hopkins. Although Hopkins was a Jesuit priest, he was inspired more by Duns Scotus than the Jesuit's official theologian Thomas Aquinas. Heidegger was also briefly a Jesuit novice and Duns Scotus thinking was the subject of his *habilitation* thesis. Hopkins invented the term 'inscape' to mean the pattern of attributes that composes the individuality of a thing and 'instress' to mean the force that binds these attributes together and, as it were, projects them into the mind of an observer. What Heidegger means by being, *das Sein*, seems to be something akin to this force. Although *Dasein* is the location of the coming-to-presence of things, the motivation is coming from the *Wesen*, the nature of things, themselves.

Heidegger assigns a safeguarding role to humanity because only human beings can sustain *Dasein* and only *Dasein* can listen to *das Sein* and intuit the *Wesen*, the essence, of things. But it is also because things have a *Wesen* that *Dasein* must be the steward and not the master. Things continue and endure; they cannot be invented. Movement is only between concealment and un-concealment. There is no room for innovation and no place for improvisation. When humanity seeks to invent, to dominate nature through science and technology for example, it only succeeds in disrupting the working of *das Sein*.

The danger from modern technological thinking, of which modern science is a component, is that it models everything as mathematical quantities, which is fine for making calculations, but disintegrates, we could say dismantles, the integrity and identity of the objects that populate the familiar world into the objectlessness of particle physics. As Heidegger puts it in *The Question Concerning Technology*:

> Thus when man, investigating, observing, ensnares nature as an area of his own conceiving, he has already been claimed by a way of revealing that challenges him to approach nature as an object of research, until even the object disappears into the objectlessness of standing-reserve.

In the transition between agrarian technology and modern technology, objects, *Gegenstände*, are disintegrated in the objectlessness of standing-reserves, *Bestande*. These objects include also ourselves of course and it is from this that Heidegger's view of the inhumanity of modern science and technology derives.

Asked in the interview *Only a God can Save Us*, recorded in 1966 but published posthumously in 1976, why it shouldn't be regarded as a good thing that scientific and technological progress leads to greater prosperity, Heidegger replied:

Everything functions. That is exactly what is uncanny. Everything functions and the functioning drives us further and further to more functioning, and technology tears people away and uproots them from the earth more and more. I don't know if you are scared; I was certainly scared when I recently saw the photographs of the earth taken from the moon. We don't need an atom bomb at all; the uprooting of human beings is already taking place. We only have purely technological conditions left. It is no longer an earth on which human beings live today.

The transition into intelligibility is motivated not by human beings but is grounded somewhere in the nature of things. The ships must leave the concealing protection of the harbour for the open seas. I cannot find in these essays any real reason why this must happen. In *The Question Concerning Technology* there is some idea of a fate, *ein Geschick.* This is characterised as both a gathering and a sending, an image that captures the idea that the fleet is marshalled and then the expedition dispatched. As with Hopkins concepts of inscape and instress, the underlying idea seems to be that what we apprehend, the familiar objects of everyday experience, are gatherings that come together in the moment of experience.

Similar ideas seem to be behind these passages from *Building, Dwelling, Thinking,* an essay from the same period, in which the idea of *being* has become the idea of *dwelling*:

Human being consists in dwelling and, indeed, dwelling in the sense of the stay of mortals on the earth. But 'on the earth' already means 'under the sky.' Both of these also mean 'remaining before the divinities' and include a 'belonging to men's being with one another.' By a primal oneness the four—earth and sky, divinities and mortals—belong together in one.

The bridge gathers to itself in its own way earth and sky, divinities, and mortals. Gathering or assembly, by an ancient word of our language, is called "thing". The bridge is a thing and, indeed, it is such as the gathering of the fourfold which we have described.

In the end, I think Heidegger recognised that his philosophical project had to be considered a failure. In *The Letter on Humanism*, published in 1947, he had already spoken of a new thinking that is to come. While the success of science and technology has put up a barrier to the apprehension of the true nature of things, in *The Question Concerning Technology* he had retained some optimism that modern science and technology would at least open a path to a better way of thinking. However, asked in the interview with *Der Spiegel* whether he was able to describe the new way of thinking that he thought was necessary, Heidegger concedes that he could not. The only hope is of some outside intervention, hence the title of the interview.

III. CONCEPTUAL THINKING

8. Skilled and unskilled intuitions

In developing my ideas over the last few years, I have been guided by two basic intuitions. The first is that conceptual structures in all domains are, fundamentally, heuristic models. The second is that the target of the application of these models is an abstraction from, rather than the totality of, reality. The two ideas are connected. Abstraction is a process of ignoring some aspects of a totality, and heuristic models are simplifications that deliberately ignore many features of their target domain.

The idea about abstraction has been with me for a long time. I think the original inspiration came from the work of Michael Oakeshott, whose postgraduate seminar at the London School of Economics I attended back in 1980. Oakeshott argued that we encounter reality in different modes, each targeted at a different abstraction. Although the scientist, the historian and the practically minded person engage with the same reality, they are engaging with it as different levels of abstraction from a common totality. The role of the philosopher in this situation is to understand the conditions that structure these diverse engagements.

The idea about model-building, on the other hand, comes from my working life as a software developer. When you build a software application, you are constructing a working model of a target domain. Developers start by asking what is, in effect, an ontological question, namely: what entities exist in the target domain and what events happen to them? In the design of the software, the structure of the entities is typically captured in the data stores and the events are coded as algorithms.

In this way of thinking, conceptualisation is based on the construction, development, application and interpretation of heuristic models. These models are heuristic in the sense that they are designed to accomplish a limited but useful task without making a claim to be unequivocal or complete. In some domains such as science, technology and finance, the models are typically quantitative and mathematical. In other domains they are predominantly categorical, meaning that they are primarily concerned with identification and classification – with what type of thing something is.

In this chapter I want to consider the nature of conceptual rationality through an analysis of the structure and application of conceptual thinking. As a starting point, it should be emphasised that conceptual thinking is not the only possible mode of thinking. There are others, including the creative, the imaginative, the contemplative and meditative, and, maybe most significantly, the associational. Associational thinking is sometimes taken to be the natural way in which the mind works, sometimes as the only way. My view is that these are all complementary; there isn't a single way of thinking.

Associational thinking works through proximity, vividness and familiarity. Conceptual thinking, on the other hand, works through structure, abstraction, type and population. Associational thinking is closely coupled to immediate experience and the appearance of things, while conceptual thinking seeks the detachment to dig below the surface.

I would resist the temptation to categorise associational thinking as irrational and conceptual thinking is rational. Both modes operate on the basis of heuristics, and heuristics tend to contain biases. The principal difference is that conceptual thinking is reflective and self-aware rather than intuitive. It is concerned not just with judgements and decision-making, but also with the basis of those judgements and decisions. This inherent concern with confirmation and evidence, with assessing the grounds of belief, also means that error detection and error correction are built into conceptual thinking in a way that they are not inherent in associational thinking.

The analysis of associational thinking goes back to the 18th century and the work of David Hume in particular. Hume, pursuing the logic of empiricism, was perhaps the first to build an idea of the mind as an engine of association. However, in this section, I want to consider one of the most important modern analyses of associational thinking, the heuristics and biases model of judgement and the prospect theory of decision-making developed by Daniel Kahneman and Aaron Tversky.

In these models, associational thinking is fast thinking, conceptual thinking slow thinking. In his book called *Thinking Fast & Slow*,

Daniel Kahneman suggests that our minds are fundamentally lazy. Thinking requires attention and effort and these capacities are easily depleted. We prefer the comfort of the familiar and coherent to the discomfort of the unfamiliar and the uncertain.

As a consequence, we tend, without being aware of it, to substitute easier questions that we can answer for harder questions that we can't. This unconscious substitution is the basis of the heuristics and biases model. In their original paper, Kahneman and Tversky identified twenty such heuristics and their associated biases.

The heuristics of unreflective thinking are carried out through the association of ideas, a process that is grounded in resemblance, proximity and the availability of information. At the same time, these heuristics contain inherent biases that lead to cognitive errors. In his book Kahneman describes how the model can be extended and developed to understand the illusions that fast thinking creates and the over-confidence that it generates.

Fast thinking is primarily a storytelling mode which automatically hunts for causes and intentions and has little understanding of logic and probability. What matters is the narrative, and the best narratives are simple and coherent. Associative reasoning works by skating over gaps in information without realising that they are there, adopting a principle that Kahneman refers to as *What you see is all there is*. It is a machine for jumping to conclusions.

The heuristic and biases model challenged then prevailing assumptions that human cognition is largely rational, and that emotions such as fear, affection and hatred explain most of the occasions when people depart from rationality. Although Kahneman concedes that emotion (that is, liking and disliking with little deliberation or reasoning) looms larger in his thinking now than it did originally, the heuristics and biases model demonstrates that simply mastering one's emotions would not by itself be sufficient to avoid cognitive error. There are unavoidable biases in the heuristics that the mind deploys in the same way that vision is subject to unavoidable optical illusion.

Fast thinking draws no clear boundary between theory and practice, between judgement formation and decision-making. Recognising such a separation would require more conscious reflection. Errors of judgements tend therefore to lead to errors in decision-making. Following on from their work on judgement, Kahneman and Tversky developed prospect theory as a descriptive psychological theory of decision-making.

The prevailing model of the rational agent, used particularly in economics, is based on postulated axioms of choice rather than observation of actual behaviour or reflection on human psychology. Behavioural economics is the outcome of attempts to bring psychological insights to economics, to take account of worry, regret, blame, anticipation and disappointment and so on as they have an impact on decision-making.

The most significant contribution of prospect theory to behavioural economics is the concept of loss aversion. The idea is that, when directly compared, losses loom larger than gains in our mental accounting. Linked to this concept is the idea that the basis of any accounting is a reference point or adaptation level, which may be the state now or an expected future state. For example, some amount of money will have a different meaning if it is an unexpected windfall rather than a disappointing shortfall from what has been anticipated. Loss aversion functions as a kind of gravitational force that holds our life together near to a set of reference points.

In the axiomatic rational agent model, outcomes are weighted by their probability. However, this turns out to be poor psychology. Emotion and the vividness of potential outcomes influence judgements of probability, which can lead to an excessive response to rare events and, in their absence, to neglect and inattention, even when the outcomes carry high stakes.

Salience is also affected by how a decision is framed. An axiomatically rational agent would make decisions about their preferences that are not affected by the words used to describe them or the context in which they are presented. But this is not how humans behave in reality. Framing effects are the unjustified influences on decisions of the formulation of beliefs and preferences, leading to decisions that become choices from description rather than choices from experience.

However, in the case of both judgements and decision-making, the irrationality of intuitive associational thinking can be overstated. Kahneman's somewhat pessimistic description of unreflective judgement and decision-making has not gone unchallenged. One alternative to the heuristics and biases model is the naturalistic decision-making model. This approach takes a more positive view of the possibility of unreflective rationality. In particular, it argues that the intuitions of experts can be better explained by prolonged practice, something Herbert Simon called intuition as recognition:

> The situation has provided a cue; this cue has given the expert access to information stored in memory, and the information provides the answer. Intuition is nothing more and nothing less than recognition.

The model also makes use of Simon's notion of satisficing, the idea that a solution may be good enough without being the best possible. Firefighters, for example, must respond quickly to developing situations and prolonged deliberation may not be possible. With expert intuition there is a high degree of probability that a good enough solution will be arrived at without prolonged deliberation of multiple options. Rather than the outcome of weighing options, decisions are made on the basis of how the situation is expected to play out.

For this reason, while intuition will always be unreflective, it is not necessarily damagingly so. In the right circumstances the intuition of experts can lead to better judgements and decisions than a more self-conscious deliberative process. It is possible with training to generate skilled intuitions and therefore execute skilled intuitive responses.

Kahneman reports that he engaged in an adversarial collaboration with Gary Klein, a leading advocate of naturalistic decision-making, to try to map the boundary between the successful acquisition of expert intuition and the flawed intuitions of associational thinking. They agreed that what is needed is both an environment that provides sufficient regularity to be reasonably predictable, as well as the opportunity to learn these regularities through prolonged practice accompanied by immediate and accurate feedback.

This argument between the heuristic and biases model and naturalistic decision-making is concerned with the strengths and weaknesses of intuitive thinking. The heuristics and biases model focuses primarily on the weaknesses; the naturalistic decision-making model places more emphasis on the strengths. However, both are evaluations of the same ability, namely, our capacity to make judgements and decisions without conscious reflection which, for that reason, become judgements and decisions that we may not be able to explain to ourselves.

However, even in regard to the heuristics and biases model, the idea that fast thinking is irrational shouldn't be overstated. Kahneman concedes that intuition gets right more than it gets wrong. Furthermore, although fast intuitive thinking is error prone, it is error prone in a systematic fashion. If you know what heuristics are being used, and what biases they are prone to, you can correct for them. The terrain of cognitive error has now been extensively mapped and a set of diagnostic labels developed, by Kahneman and others, that can be used for error detection and correction.

On the other hand, the recognition of expert intuition doesn't address the main weakness of intuitive thinking. The basic question of error detection remains. How do you find the limits of the validity of intuitive judgements and decision-making when intuition is unreflective thinking carried out below the level of conscious introspection?

The limitation of intuitive thinking is that, while it reduces the effort and time required for cognitive processing, it has no warning system to detect that it is reaching its limits and is becoming unreliable. There is no easy way to distinguish an intuitively skilled from an intuitively unskilled response. Little can be done except getting better at detecting situations where fast thinking will go wrong. The limitations of the mind don't go away. Both fast intuitive thinking and slow deliberative thinking are error prone, the difference being that slow deliberative thinking contains the error detection and correction capabilities that fast thinking doesn't have.

Furthermore, there are a couple of reasons for thinking that there is no simple solution to this problem. The first is that fast thinking isn't just a consequence of mental laziness. Heuristics are employed because, in practical judgement and decision-making, there is often too little time and too little information to come to more considered conclusions. Associational heuristics are used to navigate complex situations when time and information are in short supply. Our experience is inherently noisy and pressured.

Secondly, the faults of inattention and desire for coherence are attributes of the mind. The biases belong to the heuristics, but the aversion to ambiguity and incoherence and the tendency to over-confidence belongs to the mind, and that characteristic is discernible in every kind of thinking. Over-confidence isn't a fault of the associational heuristics of fast thinking, it is an attribute of the mind. The mind engaged in slow deliberative thinking is the same mind that is engaged in fast intuitive thinking and has the same strengths and weakness. While slow thinking contains the error detection and correction capabilities that fast thinking doesn't have, their employment depends on a willingness in the mind to accept uncertainties, limitations and ambiguity.

There is one further question concerning the interpretation of this research. Behavioural economics was developed in opposition to a particular conception of the rational agent that is prevalent in economic theory. It has puzzled me, though, that the rationality of axiomatic theories of rational choice was called into question, not because it contains a limited concept of rational choice, but because it is not applicable to the way people actually do make judgements and decisions.

However, it is not irrational to allow decisions to be impacted by emotional experience and a wider conception of wellbeing than assembling a consistent set of preferences. So, was it perhaps just easier to call into question this model by suggesting that real life judgements and decisions were irrational rather than by arguing that the concept of rationality being deployed in economics generally was mistaken?

I suspect there is a political dimension to this argument. Rational choice theory is often used to argue the case for free-market economics and against government regulation of the economy. If buyers and sellers in a marketplace are rational agents, willing and able to make their own judgements and decisions, the rationale for government regulation is significantly weakened. In this way, rational choice theory gets deployed in support of libertarian political objectives.

There are many ways to frame a counter-argument to this position. One option would be to focus on whether or not economic agents are really both able and willing agents. Economic demand is often driven by need rather than desire, and need can be exploited. There are then the question of externalities and asymmetries of information.

The behavioural approach to economic decision-making, on the other hand, has tended to focus on economic agents' abilities. Individuals, left to their own devices, make poor decisions, and for that reason, decision-making should perhaps not necessarily be left to individuals. If people think intuitively, then perhaps decision-making should be moved elsewhere, perhaps to an expert cognitive elite, who can understand better than ordinary people themselves what their best plan for life should be. This would explain why behavioural economics tends to steer towards technocratic elitism.

Before concluding this section, I wanted to take account of a different idea of intuition as recognition, one which is more closely associated with contemplative and meditative thinking. We might call this *very slow thinking.*

In this version, intuition is essentially passive rather than unreflective. What underlies this way of thinking is the idea that fundamental reality is something that can best be apprehended by the receptive mind, rather than being actively discovered; that the movement to understanding originates in the object rather than the subject; and that only when action and thought have been stilled can reality be apprehended. In this interpretation, cognition obstructs recognition.

This is an idea that has a long history. It is inherent in the classical ideal of the *vita contemplativa*, the idea of knowledge as something acquired by stilling the activity of the mind. William Wordsworth expressed this thought it in his poem *Expostulation and reply* in the collection *Lyrical Ballads*. The expostulation is addressed to a day-dreamer, and the day-dreamer's reply is:

> *Nor less I deem that there are powers,*
> *Which of themselves our minds impress,*
> *That we can feed this mind of ours,*
> *In a wise passiveness.*

The validity of this interpretation of the *vita contemplativa* depends on the validity of the ontological assumption that there is an active principal in reality, that the cosmos is trying in some way to make itself known to human understanding, and that the human mind has a supporting role in this drama and can only get in the way and obscure the truth when it tries to do something more. Heidegger was probably the most influential proponent of this idea in modern philosophy. To this way of thinking, the belief in intuition as reliable knowledge often goes with the idea that there is a reality beyond or below the appearance of the world with which the mind has an affinity and which it can know intuitively because in some way it is identified with it.

There is an alternative interpretation of this idea that doesn't require these ontological and epistemological assumptions and the consequences that flow from them. This is the idea that it is only the rational mind that should stilled, in order that the other capabilities of the mind can have sway. This is not an unattractive way of thinking. It is a useful reminder that there is a value to patient observation, and that as observers we shouldn't let ourselves get in the way of the view or impose our own perspective and concerns on the external world.

9. The category of inner and outer

As we have seen, the intellectual disciplines we are now familiar with began to take shape in the 19th century, as the natural sciences became independent disciplines, separate from natural philosophy, and the development of the social sciences led to the application of scientific methods to social institutions and individual psychology.

As discussed in section 6, Wilhelm Dilthey was one of the first philosophers to think about the implications of this development. He conceived the distinction between the *Naturwissenschaften,* the intellectual disciplines concerned with natural entities and events, and the *Geisteswissenschaften,* the intellectual disciplines concerned with social and cultural entities and events. The term *Geist* covers similar territory to the English terms *mind, culture* and *spirit,* and the *Geisteswissenschaften* include not only sociology, economics and political science but also history and archaeology, the study of religion, psychology and the theory and criticism of the arts. We don't really have a pithy equivalent in English for the term or the adjectival and adverbial qualifier *geistig.*

Dilthey proposed that these disciplines were structured according to a specific conceptual framework which was additional to the Kantian framework that applied to natural systems and structures. This framework was constructed from five conceptual categories: parts and wholes, means and ends, value, power, and inner and outer. It is this last category that is the most innovative and important.

The category of parts and wholes is the question of composition. The underlying idea here is that complexity is not analysable. Dilthey had in mind the difficulties of interpretation, where a whole, such as a text, could only be understood in terms of the words and phrases of which it was composed but, at the same time, the meaning of the words and phrases can only be understood in terms of the text as a whole, setting up what he called a hermeneutic or interpretative circle. The original impetus towards the concept of a hermeneutic circle came from contemporary developments in archaeology and the interpretation of ancient texts. It's arguable that the idea that complexity isn't analysable applies also to the natural sciences. However, the tools to model complex systems weren't developed until a century later. In the 19th century, the prevailing idea was that science was engaged in the discovery of causal necessity and the laws of nature.

The next three categories are fairly straightforward. The category of means and ends is the idea of instrumentality, the idea that actions are undertaken to achieve an objective or outcome; the category of value is the idea that objectives and outcomes matter to participants; and the category of power is the idea that participants in a course of events are not passengers but active agents, initiating, and understanding themselves to be initiating, a course of action and setting in train a sequence of events with the purpose of achieving a desirable goal.

Dilthey's final category is the distinction between inner and outer. We don't understand natural events as the outward expression of an inner life. Instead, we explain them, from the outside, as the outcome of regularities in the way natural systems and structures evolve under a given set of constraints. If you remove the plug, the water in a tank will drain away, without the need to project an inner life onto either the water or the tank.

In the social sciences and the humanities, on the other hand, we do understand entities and events as the outward expression of an inner life. This is how Dilthey expresses it in his major work, *The Formation of the Historical World in the Human Studies*:

> At this point the meaning of the concepts inner and outer and the justification for using them becomes clear. They designate the relationship which exists in the understanding between the outer phenomena of life and what produces them and is expressed in them. The relationship between inner and outer exists only for understanding, just as the relationship between phenomena and that by which they are explained exists only for scientific cognition.

There are a couple of points to think about here. The first is the degree to which the presence or absence of an interior life is an ontological difference rather than an epistemological and logical framing. The Kantian model tends to suggest that it is a different way of knowing, rather than a different way of being, and that Dilthey was not proposing a dualist ontology in the Cartesian mode. The distinction is based on the observer's concerns and so leaves open the question whether there is an underlying ontological distinction.

However, it's doubtful that this is sustainable position. Although the paradigm tends to focus on the way in which the observer frames the experience, it's difficult to see how the possession of an inner life can't be an ontological difference. Treating a cultural event as a natural event will generate failures of explanation, just as treating a natural event as a cultural event will generate failures of understanding, because in both cases the epistemology and logic isn't congruent with the ontology of the target domain.

Although this framework is cognizant of the inner life of the participants, it is still the view from the outside, and in that sense, remains continuous with the natural sciences and philosophy. There was another strand in Dilthey's thinking, in which he developed his ideas about lived experience. Lived experience engages not only with meaning but also with value, purpose and consequence; the sense that our current state is a consequence of prior actions and events. It was this strand of Dilthey's thinking that influenced the development of Husserl's phenomenology, the *Existenzphilosophie* of Heidegger and Karl Jaspers and later the development of existentialism in France, all of which were concerned with understanding experience from the inside.

One limitation of the concept of *Geisteswissenschaften* is that it doesn't clearly distinguish between the social sciences and the humanities. In the course of discussing the work on inequality of the economist Thomas Piketty in the *London Review of Books*, William Davies succinctly brings out the nature of this distinction and points to the opportunities created by bringing together the two different sets of disciplines:

> *One conventional distinction between the social sciences and the humanities is that the humanities explore artefacts produced by people (novels, documents, letters, political tracts), while the social*

sciences generate new empirical facts about people through various quantitative and qualitative methods. As Savage notes, Piketty's work bridges the divide, and not just because he brings Austen and Balzac into his economic analyses. By turning to the archives for material, rather than survey instruments or orthodox inequality measures such as the Gini coefficient, Piketty presents the problem of inequality afresh, using new forms of historical narration and explanation that cut across disciplines and theoretical frameworks.

The relation of parts and wholes is one dimension of the open-endedness of interpretation. There is in addition the question of reflexivity and recursion, which contribute an additional dimension to complexity and the instability of interpretation: the inner life of the participant which the outside observer seeks to understand will be informed by the same conceptual framework that the theorist is employing. The evolution of the cultural framework driven by the observer's desire to understand will itself become part of the cultural framework within which participants make judgements and decisions.

The category of inner and outer can be applied to the way that intellectual and practical disciplines are classified. Modern intellectual life is characterised by a high degree of specialisation. This is reflected, for example, in the way that university faculties are organised around the distinctions between the natural sciences, the social sciences and the humanities. To this is added the distinction between pure and applied disciplines. If we also take account of the more formal and abstract disciplines, we get a fourfold classification. The examples given here are intended only to illustrate the categories – they are not meant to be exhaustive.

Firstly, there are the theoretical disciplines concerned with natural systems and structures:

- Physics, chemistry, the biological and the Earth sciences.

Nature, as the target domain of the natural sciences, is imagined as independent of any conceptual structure or practical application and there is no temptation to suppose that the outward behaviour of a natural system is the expression of an interior life.

Secondly, there are theoretical disciplines concerned with human experience, culture and society:

- Disciplines concerned with societies and institutions: sociology, economics, political science;
- Disciplines concerned with individuals: psychology;
- Disciplines concerned with the past: history, archaeology; and
- Disciplines concerned with cultural artefacts: the humanities.

Although they are concerned with the human actions and projects, these disciplines aren't constructed from the interior point-of-view. Rather, they are based on the point-of-view of an observer intuiting that what they are observing and seeking to understand is the outward manifestation of the inner thoughts and motivations of self-aware, though not necessarily insightful, participants. These inner motivations may not necessarily have a connection to objective reality. The view from outside must try to interpret the outward appearance for clues to the inner movement – which may or may not have reliable insight into itself.

The third group of disciplines is concerned with theory as the basis for action. In these disciplines a theoretical understanding is married to a practical purpose. They are therefore shaped by the participant's point-of-view, purposes, interests and values:

- Disciplines concerned with production: engineering, design;
- Disciplines concerned with therapy: medicine, psychoanalysis;
- Disciplines concerned with organisation & strategy: public and business administration, law; and
- Disciplines concerned with creativity: the literary, visual & performing arts.

Engineering disciplines draw on an understanding of forces and materials in order to construct the built environment. Similarly, medicine draws on an understanding of biology, chemistry and physics, but does so from a perspective that is concerned with human wellbeing and the diagnosis and treatment of ill-health.

Finally, there is a fourth group of theoretical disciplines which are concerned with very abstract conceptual models, with thinking about thinking:

- Disciplines concerned with formal structure: logic, mathematics;

- Disciplines concerned with cognition: epistemology; and
- Disciplines concerned with existence: ontology.

These formalisms apply to any discipline – and not just to intellectual disciplines, but any structured practice or activity. In each case, there is an ontology, an inventory of entities and events; a logic, in the sense of an approach to giving an account; and an epistemology, an account of what it means to know something in the target domain. The epistemology connects the logic to the ontology. Metaphysics is these categories at the most abstract level, where the application is not limited to a specific domain, but applies to everything, everywhere, and all times.

There is one further distinction I want to set-up before considering conceptual thinking. This is the distinction between individuation, which is an ontological idea, and individuality, which is a logical idea. Individuation is concerned with separation and integration, with answering the question, why is there a discernible *this* here, while individuality is concerned with what type of thing this *this* is, its *somethingness*.

10. Individuation, individuality & typicality

There are two sides to the concept of an individual entity, which might be called individuation and individuality. These have quite different dynamics and consequences. Individuation is the fundamental premise of ontology. Even if there is only one entity, and all is one, that entity will still be individuated. Individuality, and its counterpart typicality, are a matter of logic. Typicality and individuality, the degree to which an object conforms to or diverges from a type, are the fundamental premises of logic.

Everything is individuated in some way, whether it is a single drop of water or the universe in its entirety. Individuation is a matter of separation and integration, and therefore also of identity. Both separation and integration are necessary to singularity. For something to be singular, it needs to be not only separated from its environment but also internally integrated. For an entity to be individuated, there must be at the same time both a partitioning of some domain into separate entities and, at the same time, a degree of integration which places a limit on further separation. Partitioning generates individual entities which further partitioning would dissolve. The logic is therefore that an individuated entity is the outcome of a balance between the forces of separation and the forces of integration. Separative forces tend to the dissolution of entities, integrative forces to their continuance.

Individuation is connected to identity through time. Every individuated entity has a lifetime, which lasts from the initial moment of separation and integration until there is a loss of separateness or disintegration. The balance of the forces of separation and integration will determine the stability and resilience of the individuated entity and the possibility of its persistence through time.

Individuality, on the other hand, is a question of sameness and difference in structure, function and patterns of evolution. Individuality is a matter of classification and type: what is more typical is less individual and what is more individual is less typical. Individuality is therefore sensitive to the level of abstraction, so that components that are homogeneous at one level can be heterogeneous at another. The more abstract the category, the less scope there is for individuality.

This distinction between individuation and individuality is coded into language. Individuation is adverbial. It is the where, when, why and how of things. Individuality, in contrast, is adjectival and is concerned with the what of things.

There is a spectacular diversity of types of entity in the world but, at a high level of abstraction, four basic patterns of individuation can be identified. I will call them structures, systems, substances and populations. This typology is derived from two features of the components of an entity, the level of cohesion and the level of homogeneity.

In this typology, structures are relatively cohesive entities built from components of different kinds. They are typically modular. A modular structure is a whole constructed from a number of parts. Unfortunately, we don't have a familiar word for the product of such modular construction: the components are modules and the construction is modular, but there isn't a precise word for the end result.

There are two basic kinds of structure, the mechanical and the organic. The difference is that mechanical structures are assembled: the parts are constructed separately and then the whole is put together from the component parts. For this reason, the components of a mechanical structure can be highly diverse in form, material and function.

In contrast, organic structures grow such that additional components are formed through processes of extension, division and differentiation rather than through processes of assembly. The parts don't exist prior to the whole; rather, the whole extends, divides and diversifies. Organic structures often appear highly differentiated, but looked at more closely, there is a repetition of patterns and materials.

This distinction between mechanical and organic is concerned with the composition rather than the components. Living organisms are organic structures in this sense, but the more basic components of organic structures such as proteins, carbohydrates and nucleic acids are mechanical structures. Human artefacts are typically mechanical in construction.

Distribution of function is a characteristic of both mechanical and organic structures. Functions that support the whole are distributed among the components, with each component performing a task for the benefit of the whole. Each component has a role within the whole and there is usually a central component which functions to communicate, co-ordinate and control the operation of each component.

Systems, like structures, are characterised by the diversity of their components. However, where structures are characterised by a distribution of function, systems are characterised by distribution of control. In a system, each component functions and evolves according to its own organising principles. There is no coordinating or controlling centre. The consequence is that the system evolves through the interaction, adaptation, and mutual accommodation of its components.

Substances and populations differ from structures and systems in that their components are homogeneous rather than heterogeneous. Both structures and systems are composed of heterogeneous components, the difference between them being the level of cohesion. Structures are relatively cohesive, systems relative loose. This same distinction can be applied to substances and populations: substances are relatively cohesively bound together, populations relatively loosely.

By substance, I am thinking of what we usually mean by material substances such as water, oxygen, limestone and so on. The modern idea of a substance was first articulated in 1794 by the chemist Joseph Proust. A substance has a constant composition, so that any sample of that substance will have the same composition as any other sample.

We don't usually think of substances as being individuated, but they are; what we encounter are samples of substances. Taking water as an example, some of these samples, such as oceans and rivers, are large and enduring, others, such as puddles and raindrops, are small and evanescent. Some substances are collections of small and highly undifferentiated objects such as grains of sand and seeds, and are weighed rather than counted, even though they are composed of individuated grains.

The relation between a population and a substance is analogous to the relation between system and structure. What distinguishes a substance from a population is the level of cohesion. Substances are characterised by organisation. As an example, both ice and water can be thought of as substances because the molecules are organised into a structure. When water evaporates, however, the molecules lose structure, becoming a gas.

This kind of population can be thought of as a *population through proximity*. Substances will become populations by proximity though the loss of cohesion – such as when grains of sand are dispersed by a breeze. Conversely, populations through proximity can become substances as the density of the components increases and the component elements become aggregated.

There is another kind of population, which I will call a *population by resemblance*. A population by resemblance is a conceptual construct and doesn't necessarily map to an individuated entity or event. It is a classificatory construction, and the entities that fall within the classification may have no relationship or interaction with each other. For example, pine trees in a forest form a population through proximity whereas pine trees as a class form a population through resemblance. A population through resemblance is a class or type rather than an entity. Populations by proximity may transition into populations by resemblance and vice versa, as a population by proximity that continues to disperse will eventually become a population by resemblance, and a population by resemblance that coheres will become a population by proximity, but a population by resemblance may never have been a population by proximity.

Although individuated entities may enjoy only a fleeting existence, like a puddle of water after rain, a pattern typically persists through time, implying both diachronic and synchronic identity. For an object to have diachronic identity, the evolution of the entity must happen in a way that maintains both its separation and its integration throughout its lifecycle, from the time at which the components are originally brought together until the time at which they are finally dissolved and dispersed.

Change in all entities happens both internally, in a reconfiguration of the existing components, and externally, with an exchange of components across the entity boundary, as components enter from or depart to the environment. Entities in which there is a distribution of control can more easily support an exchange of components with the external world because there is much less interdependency of components. Entities in which there is a distribution of function, on the other hand, will be much more vulnerable to the exchange of components because of their integrated functional dependency.

There isn't a clear demarcation line between structures and systems or substances and populations, or indeed between cohesive and loose entities. Many entities will have a degree of distribution of function and a degree of distribution of control and the same entity can often, depending on the focus of attention, be regarded as a structure or a system.

Furthermore, establishing identity through time is not always straightforward. What is it that leads us to think we have just the one entity at different times rather than two? There are two ways of thinking about continuity of identity through change. Firstly, there is identity in terms of composition, which might be called *compositional identity*. Although almost every entity is composite, the churn of components as old components becoming worn out and dropped and new components are added means that few entities have compositional identity throughout their lifetime.

The second form of identity through time is identity in terms of pattern and process, something that could be called *process identity*. Process identity comes into play once components can enter and leave across the entity boundary. Rivers makes a good model for process identity. The water in the river is constantly flowing, but we can reasonably say that it is the same river because, even though it is constantly changing in terms of composition, it nevertheless flows from the same source to the same destination between the same banks. While most entities, including human beings, have both kinds of identity, process identity is usually more significant than component identity. Process identity can include changes of form as well as changes of content and configuration.

Process identity can stretch a long way, but not infinitely. Most entities have a defined lifecycle. Components are gathered together to form an entity, retained or recycled during its lifecycle, and eventually dispersed when the entity disintegrates. The process that binds a set of components to form an individual entity in the first place may not be the same process that maintains the entity throughout its evolution.

Individuation is more fundamental than individuality; it has both priority in time and in salience. The members of even the most uniform population will pick up a distinctiveness, if only from having a particular history. Individuation tends to lead to individualisation, but individuality presupposes individuation. Individuated entities occupy a unique location in space and time and therefore exist in a unique relation to everything else. Even the most undifferentiated individuated entities will stand in their own unique relationship to the world around them and experience a particular history, acquiring a level of individuality.

11. Conceptual structures

A conceptual structure has two components, a single conceptual schema and a set of conceptual objects. The conceptual schema specifies the type while the set of conceptual objects allows for the specification of particular instantiations of the type. The two components are tied together; the schema is the set of attributes that describe the type, while the object contains the values associated with those attributes that describe an instantiation of the type, that is, a specific entity or event.

Because they have no values, conceptual schemas have structure but not state. A conceptual schema can apply to or represent a type of object because of a commonality of structure, but it can't represent an actual object, because an actualised object always has a state as well as a structure. A conceptual object, on the other hand, has both structure and state; the structure is inherited from the schema, and the state is specified by the values associated with the attributes of the structure. Actual entities and events can only be represented by conceptual objects, because only conceptual objects have a state.

I have borrowed this distinction between conceptual schema and conceptual objects from the practice of software development. Schemas specify the form in which information is to be organised. The schemas describe the classes or types of objects that can be processed by the software, what attributes they have, what domain of values the contents of the attributes are drawn from, and what rules are in place to validate that the structure has valid content. Usually, in a software application, there will be database schemas that specify the structure of the data stores and message schemas that specify the structure of the messages sent and received by the components of the system.

The advantage of thinking in these terms is that conceptual structure can be analysed as a piece of engineering. Like software applications, conceptual structures are working models of a target domain, and conceptual thinking is in that sense an engineering discipline.

There is also a philosophical precedent for this use of the term. As discussed earlier in section 4 of this essay, Kant, in the *Critique of Pure Reason,* argues that our internal representation of the world that we experience empirically through the senses is shaped by our non-empirical intuitions of time and space, together with certain non-empirical categories of thought. There are twelve of these categories, organised under four headings: quantity, quality, relation and modality. A set of rules associated with each of the twelve categories allows the understanding to generate a set of terms or concepts, and the reason can then join subject concepts to predicate concepts to form judgements.

The set of rules Kant calls *schemas.* They are a kind of procedure through which the understanding constructs the conceptual framework which is turned by reasoning into judgements. The schemas associated with each of the twelve categories are required in order for the mind to make sense of experience. The categories are the condition that allows the mind to unify moments of sensory experience into a single integrated representation of the world that can be understood and reasoned about. For this reason, Kant considered them to be *a priori,* imposed on experience rather than derived from it.

Kant considered this insight to represent an intellectual achievement equivalent to Copernicus's revolution. The first revolution had been to move the centre of the cosmos from the Earth, where it had been in the Ptolemaic system, to the sun. This second revolution was to move the definition of things from the object, where it had been in the Aristotelian system, into the subject of cognizance.

However, in the model that I am proposing, these very abstract categories are artefacts of conceptual structure rather than functions either of reality or of the activity of the mind. The reason is that wherever you start from and whatever target domain of application you are considering, the process of abstraction will always terminate with the same set of ideas. Conceptual schemas are organised into type-hierarchies (hierarchies of abstraction), and at the top level of any and every conceptual schema there will always be the same ultimate abstractions. At the apex there will be the very abstract concepts of entity and event and their attributes, and for this reason I would argue that these categories are a function of abstraction rather than products of the human mind or attributes of reality. In that sense, abstraction is a process of discovery, not invention.

Associated with *entity* and *event* will be a further set of attributes. The conception of an *entity* implies *boundary, extent, location* and *state*; the conception of an *event* implies *sequence, duration and change of state*. Both *entity* and *event* imply *type* and *type* in turn implies *abstraction* and *instantiation*. Moreover, *instantiation* implies *population, actuality* and *possibility*. As this chain of concepts suggests, there is always a significant amount of structure behind even the simplest conceptual thought.

What is meant by rules of interpretation for the construction of concepts? There are a number of strategies available with regard to the representation of abstract concepts; strategies such as analogues, proxies and placeholders. In my mind, for example, the placeholder for the concept *entity* looks like a blob drawn on a page, an irregular line which closes in a loop. Because the loop creates a boundary and therefore an extent, a location and a state, a structure is produced that can be projected topologically onto any other structure as an analogue, a kind of overlay or map, turning the image of the target from the representation of a specific entity into a representation of the abstraction *entity*.

Similarly, with regard to *events*, I tend to think of the image of a switch as a proxy. A switch is any entity that has only two possible states: on and off; up or down; one or zero; and so on. Therefore, the only possible events or changes of state applicable to a switch are to toggle between these two states. In this case, simplicity is a proxy for abstraction. This very abstract model of a change of state can also be projected mentally onto any other change of state to turn it into the representation of the abstraction *event*.

In a type-hierarchy, the sub-types inherit attributes from the parent types, so that the sub-type has all the attributes of the parent type plus the attributes that are specific to the sub-type. This means that sub-types are less abstract: they specify an entity or event more extensively.

At each level in the hierarchy there are attributes that characterise the entity at that level of abstraction. For example, if *cellular-composition* is a characteristic of living organisms, *cell-walls-containing-cellulose* is a characteristic of plants and *supported-on-a-rigid-stem-or-trunk* is a characteristic of trees. Families of trees are in turn distinguished by their characteristic attributes. As an example, oaks are a sub-type of tree, trees are a sub-type of plants, and plants are a sub-type of living organisms. The sub-type at each level of abstraction inherits the attributes of all the higher levels of abstraction, so oak trees inherit the characteristics of trees generally, and also of plants, of living organisms, and ultimately of entities.

A simple term in a sentence, such as *this oak tree*, may appear simply to tag an instance of a particular type of tree, but it brings with it not only the attributes and values that specify oak trees, but also the attributes and values that specify trees, plants, living organisms and, at the apex, contains the basic idea about the individuation of entities and events.

For every entry in a type-hierarchy there is a matching hierarchy of populations by resemblance. There is an inverse relationship between the level of abstraction of the type and the size of the matching population: the fewer the defining attributes there are in the type, the larger will be the population of objects that the type will apply to. This means that the more abstract the type, the larger the population and, conversely, the more extensive the type, the smaller the population that it will apply to. In my example, the population of oaks is smaller than the population of trees, the population of trees is smaller than the population of plants, and the population of plants is smaller than the population of living organisms.

There are many conceptual hierarchies of this kind and any entity can belong to multiple hierarchies. Abstraction isn't excluding.

In this example, oak trees have been considered in terms of form, function and composition, but the botanical classification will be made in terms of evolutionary relationships. The type-hierarchy for a human being might run *human being—living organism—entity* if you are concerned with the biological being, and *person—being—entity* if you are concerned with the subjective, cultural and social being.

The same analysis applies to events. An event, at the most abstract level, is a change of state. Entities and events are linked in that an event is a change in the state of an entity. For example, accompanying the entity hierarchy *plant—living organism—entity* we might have the event hierarchy *photosynthesis—metabolic process—event*. Modelling in terms of entities creates the synchronic perspective on a target domain, one which describes the state of the entity at a moment in time, whereas modelling in terms of events creates the diachronic perspective, one which describes changes in the state of an entity through time.

There are many forms in which conceptual structure can be rendered: words, equations, functions, maps, graphs, charts, tables, diagrams, sketches and so on; and most conceptual structures can be rendered in more than one form. However, the two most important forms are language and mathematics. Conceptual structure and the distinction between schema and object are present in both, but it is perhaps more obvious in mathematics. Indeed, the structure of natural language tends to obscure rather than exhibit the underlying structure of concepts.

In natural language, a statement is a string of terms representing classes or types of entity and event which forms a judgement, statement or proposition. Such a statement, without quantification or qualification, represents a generalisation about all entities and events that map to these types: birds fly; fish swim; people think, and so on. This is reflected in the stipulation in formal English grammar that only a statement containing both a subject and a verb can be considered a sentence. Lacking either, it's just a fragment of one.

There are a number of mechanisms that can be used to restrict the domain of application: adjectival and adverbial qualifiers and quantifiers, pointers, and names. The use of these can narrow down the reference to a subset of the population of entities that maps to a class, possibly even to an individual. It's also possible that the specification is restricted sufficiently that there is no domain of application.

Descriptions are formed from the set of qualifiers and quantifiers applied to types. The basic quantifiers are *none, some* and *all*. There is a wide range of adjectival and adverbial qualifiers. For example, in the statement *The note on the desk was missing,* the phrase *on the desk* is an adverbial qualifier that narrows down the reference. Qualification and quantification are very context sensitive. This statement will be sufficient if there has been only one note on the desk.

For this reason, qualification and quantification are often accompanied by pointers. The most basic are *this* and *that, here* and *there, now* and *then*. Pronouns can also serve as pointers. We recognise that *I* and *you* and *they* point to different persons depending on the context.

The third linguistic mechanism is the use of names. A name is a label. The problem with descriptions and pointers is that they are vulnerable to change. If we are describing a book, and we try to reference it by saying it is the one *on the table*, that may be fine in a very narrow framing, but not if there is time for someone to move or replace it. The idea with names is that they are a label that remains constant through changes of state. The disadvantage of names is that they depend on both parties to a communication already knowing what the name refers to.

In natural language, a statement without qualifiers, quantifiers, pointers or names will describe a conceptual schema – *a relation of ideas*, in Hume's terminology. A statement which includes these will define a set of conceptual objects, and those conceptual objects may map to a population of actual objects, a population of zero, one or many.

Mathematical statements don't have the same implicit addressing mechanisms, so the link between schema and domain of application has to be made explicitly. One of the features of mathematics is that the same mathematical object can have multiple domains of application. For example, it would not make sense to use the same natural language to describe the relationship between the model of a projectile in flight and the model of marginal cost in business, but the same mathematical analysis, calculus, because it is concerned with the rates of change in a quantity, can be applied to both.

Conceptual structure is the basis of conceptual thinking. By abstracting attributes and values from the totality of things, we can build a type, and understand objects as instances of types. This process of abstraction and classification allows us to obtain new knowledge about things.

There are two basic methods. The logical method is to find new knowledge by pursuing the inferences that can be drawn from the application of the conceptual structure. If the conceptual structure applies to some actual structures, then the relationships in the conceptual structure can be used to draw conclusions about the actual structures. The scientific method is used to find new knowledge about things through techniques of categorisation and quantification, so that we can arrive at generalisations about populations, which will apply, within a set of constraints, to individual entities within those populations.

There is one further point to make. Conceptual schemas are themselves composite objects, so it is also necessary to have a conceptual meta-schema which describes how the schemas are to be specified. Conceptual schemas are themselves the conceptual objects of a meta-schema, which means that while a conceptual schema is stateless when considered in relation to conceptual objects, it does describe a state, when considered in relation to the meta-schema. Happily, as meta-schemas are self-referential, there is no need for a meta-meta-schema to describe the meta-schema.

12. A manifesto for heuristic modelling

In his book *A Brief History of Time*, Stephen Hawking described the practice of scientific theorising in this way:

> *A theory is just a model of the universe...and a set of rules that relate quantities in the model to observations that we make. A theory is a good theory if it satisfies two requirements: it must accurately describe a large class of observations on the basis of a model that contains only a few arbitrary elements, and it must make definite predictions about the results of future observations.*

The first part of Hawking's requirement of a good scientific theory re-iterates the criteria of scope and simplicity that were previously put forward by the neo-Kantians and by Thomas Kuhn and, as discussed in section 3, were invoked by Descartes back at the beginnings of the Scientific Revolution. These criteria are common to theories in all domains. It is the second part, the requirement to make definite, empirically testable predictions, that distinguishes science from metaphysics. However, while scientific theories must be empirically testable, science as a discipline has to be evaluated critically using much the same criteria as metaphysics and, indeed, every other discipline.

While not all science is mathematical, models in physics, the foundational science, are essentially mathematical. The current state of a physical system, its predicted future state, and the experimental evidence that confirms the prediction are all described in mathematical terms. For this reason, our familiar intuitions and concepts usually aren't sufficient to understand them. As Roger

Penrose put it in the interview cited earlier:

> And then you say, well what is an electron? And what's a quark? And
> at that stage, the best you can do is to describe some mathematical
> structure...you say, they're things that satisfy the Dirac equation, or
> something like that...which you can't understand what that means,
> without mathematics.

The core message of this chapter on conceptual thinking is that the proper form of language is not *X is y* but *X satisfies the concept y*. This removes the persistent ambiguity between expressions of identification, attribution and classification and expressions of existence that has plagued philosophical thinking from the beginning. It also makes clear that there are two commensurable statements: *X exists,* meaning *X is a discernible object, entity or event,* and *Y exists,* meaning *Y is a conceptual structure,* and there always remains the possibility that *There is no y that is satisfied by x,* and *There is no x that satisfies y.* Language relates to the world contingently, not essentially.

The formal mathematical expression of physical structures should be distinguished from the interpretations that accompany them. There are more than twenty different interpretations of quantum physics, reflecting, in many cases, fundamentally different philosophical assumptions. There are different tests that can be applied to assess the cogency of these interpretations – those tests of scope, simplicity, coherence, consistency, adequacy, absence of arbitrariness, and necessity previously discussed – but the interpretations are not properly empirical scientific theories in Hawking's sense.

What, then, is a model in science and mathematics? In *Theory and Practice*, his introduction to the philosophy of science, Peter Godfrey-Smith provides this general description of a conceptual model:

> *...we might think of a model as a structure that is intended to represent another structure by virtue of an abstract similarity relationship between them.*

> *Mathematical models are attempts to represent relationships that might exist between the components of the real system which is its target:*

> *A mathematical model will treat one variable as a function of others, which in turn are functions of others, and so on. In this way, a complicated network of dependence structures can be represented. And then, via a commentary, the dependence structure in the model can be treated as representing the dependence structure that might exist in a real system.*

> *Such models bring an important flexibility to scientific work. Different scientists can interpret the same model in different ways:*

> *One person might use the model as a predictive device, something that gives an output when you plug in specific inputs, without caring how the inner workings of the model relate to the real world. Another person might treat the same model as a highly detailed picture of the dependence structure inside the real system being studied. And there is a range of possible attitudes between these two extremes; another person might treat the model as*

representing some features, but only a few, of what is going on in the real system.

As this suggests, scientific and mathematical models are not simply a representation of structure; they also capture the way in which structures evolve. They are working models of a target domain.

However, while actualised entities evolve, conceptual objects cannot change state, and the evolution of an actual entity must be simulated by a sequence of conceptual objects. In order to track the evolution of the real-world object, this evolution has to be simulated at the conceptual level, and this simulation is accomplished by using algorithms. An algorithm is a series of instructions for a set of actions which changes the values of the attributes of the conceptual object, so that it continues to map to the state of the real-world entity. By applying an algorithm to the state of the conceptual object, it can be turned into a working model of the real-world entity. This is much like a film: the images appear to be in motion, but in fact the effect has been simulated by running a sequence of still images through a projector at an appropriate speed.

Events are changes in state. Only actual entities can change state. A conceptual object can apply to or represent the evolution of a real-world entity only by mapping the algorithmic evolution of the conceptual objects state to the evolution of the state of the entity. In scientific models, this is almost always a matter of functions. A mathematical function is a statement of dependency between two or more variables. Functions can represent both the synchronic state of a number of entities or the change of state of one entity through time.

In modern physics, the most significant equations are differential equations, which is an equation that expresses a dependency between the rate of change in an independent variable to the rate of change in a dependent variable. This is how the physicist Leonard Susskind puts it:

> [Current physics] almost always has to do with differential equations. Let me take back one phrase: almost. It always has to do with differential equations, yes. It may be that other mathematical things are more important than the differential equations in this particular area or that particular area, but it always has to do with differential equations.

Real-world entities have a state and that state evolves through time. A mathematical object such as function doesn't itself change state, but because the set of objects in a function can represent moments in time, the evolution of a physical system can be represented by a mathematical function.

The second significant feature of a heuristic model is its level of abstraction. Models are intended to be abstract. Abstraction is a process of understanding that creates conceptual models that can be applied to reality, firstly in order to recognise and identify and, secondly, in order to understand and explain. Our ability to makes rational sense of the world to a large extent depends on how far the generalisations applicable to an abstract type capture the possibilities that inhere in an individuated totality. Our understanding will be limited by the scale of the gap between type and instance.

Both conceptual schemas and conceptual objects map to abstractions from actual entities and events. Abstraction is a process in which some features of a totality are ignored. A conceptual schema has form but not content and can therefore only map to another abstraction without content. A conceptual object, on the other hand, has both form and content, and can map to an abstraction that also has both form and content.

Abstraction in everyday use can mean a number of different things. In one meaning it is the contrary of *concrete*, in the way that we might talk about a population of human beings sharing a common humanity, where the population is concrete and the humanity is an abstraction. The underlying idea in this conception is that abstractions cannot exist independently, but are attributes of something concrete.

However, a second meaning, and the one I have in mind, is abstraction as the contrary of totality. Abstraction in this sense is the picking out of certain characteristics for attention. In this meaning, *human being* is an abstraction. Our object of attention as a totality has many attributes, but most of them we ignore most of the time, picking out only those that are significant at the time. In this sense, *plant* is more abstract than *tree*, but both conceptions apply to the same target object.

There is a gradient to the level of abstraction. A representation that was a totality would be at one end of the scale of abstraction. I don't believe it is practically possible to represent the totality of an entity, but even if it were possible, a model that wasn't an abstraction from a totality would have little value, like a map that was on the same scale as the terrain. At the other end of this scale are the most abstract of all concepts, the concepts of state and change of state, of entity and event.

The connection between conceptual modelling and abstraction is that models are heuristic in function. They are intended to accomplish a limited but useful task by simplifying the representation of an actual system or structure, and abstraction is the means by which this useful function is achieved.

Reflecting on the success of mathematical modelling in physics, in the interview cited above, Susskind echoes Roger Penrose:

> *Why is it so hard to explain physics in the English language? The intuitions and the concepts that we evolved with are not sufficient to understand them. In trying to explain it to people who don't have the mathematical background, we get stuck.*

What are these intuitions and concepts that create barriers to understanding mathematics and physics in familiar language? It's not just a matter of concision and precision, although these are significant. It's also not just that the wider public has less knowledge of mathematics, because that begs the question why this should be so: the language of mathematics is in some ways much simpler than natural language, the syntax has fewer components and the semantic content is much more restricted.

It's more likely to be a question of the intuitions and concepts that have evolved with natural languages. As Godfrey-Smith notes:

Models have a different kind of representational relationship with the world from that found in language...

in thinking about how a mathematical model might succeed in representing the world, the linguistic concepts of truth, falsity, reference, and so forth do not seem to be useful...

Some would add that even when we are dealing with language, the concepts of truth and reference might be bad ones to use.

Why might this be? Truth and reference appear to be closely connected, since the intuitive idea of truth is that there is some level of correspondence between the terms in a statement and the nature and relationships of the structure which is its target – what it is about.

However, there are differing ideas about what it means for something to be true. Modern analytic philosophy tends to assume the correspondence theory of truth. In the philosophy of mind, propositions are the units of analysis; mental contents are propositions, mental states are attitudes to propositions and mental activity is the evolution of a set of propositions and propositional attitudes. Propositions have intentionality (they are about something), and true propositions have some valid relationship to what they are about, while false propositions don't. Structuralists and critical theorists, on the other hand, tend to the view that truth lies primarily in the coherence of a structure of discourse rather than its relationship to reality and American pragmatism tends to the view that truth is a function of successful engagement with reality; truth is what works from a point of view and agenda.

As you might expect in an essay advocating pluralism, my view is that these theories have explanatory purchase within a restricted domain of application but are only partial accounts of the global picture.

That global picture has a number of layers: experience, representation, conceptualisation, discourse and critical rationality. Experience is the moment-to-moment stream of sensations, feelings, attitudes and emotions. Representations are our stable internal maps of the world. Both experience and representation include language. Conceptualisation is the self-conscious and language-dependent picking out of repetitions and patterns in these sensations and representations, classifying, analysing and labelling them in order to build conceptual models. A discourse is the assessment of the way that conceptual models fit together, expressed in descriptions and propositions. Discourses can be at different scales, from the diagnostic and forensic attention to a particular case, to the entirety of an intellectual or practical discipline. Finally, reflective and critical rationality is the mind turning its attention to conceptualisation itself, and to the understanding, explanation and justification of the whole structure.

The dynamics of this structure are not linear or even circular. It is an example of what Wilhelm Dilthey called a *Wirkungszusammenhang*, the outcome of the interaction of multiple dynamics originating from multiple sources each with its own logic. Each component evolves according to its internal logic while at the same time adapting to the evolution of the surrounding components of the system, which form its functional horizon.

The strength of structuralist and pragmatist ideas of truth and reference comes from a focus on the scale of discourse, discipline and practice. There isn't really a sense in which an intellectual discipline such as physics or biology or a practical discipline such as medicine or engineering is true or false. However, that doesn't mean we can't step outside these discourses and correct them from the outside. They aren't sealed from external influence, and their evolution will adapt not only to remedy internal incoherence but also take into account inputs from experience mediated through representation, wider conceptual change, and continuing critical reflection.

Similarly, reductivist and analytical ideas of truth and reference have most force when considering particular experiences and representations. What tends to change is not the report of the experience but its significance and interpretation. So, for example, it seems unlikely that the measurement of the speed of light, or the shape of the Earth, will change, but it would be surprising if a future physics didn't interpret these observations within a different framework. Similarly, while it seems unlikely that we will suddenly discover that life doesn't evolve, it is quite likely that future theories of biological evolution will look different from the current ones.

The idea behind conceptual modelling is that a conceptual model has a domain of application rather than a reference, and the relationship is one of applicability rather than truth or falsehood. This has a number of advantages. Applicability has a bagginess that reference doesn't have. It can be loose enough when required to cope with imprecisions and multiplicity, and strict enough at other times when rigour is looked for. It avoids the binary nature of the true /

false distinction, recognising the multiplicity of possible conceptual models. It also recognises the significance of levels of abstraction, so that one object can be conceptualised in many different ways, depending on the level of abstraction.

Back in the 14th century, William of Ockham argued that we have an intuitive apprehension of an object's existence separately from our recognition of its type or form. The subject–predicate structure of language has always tended to obscure this. It is actually quite difficult to articulate existence without presuming classification – to avoid, without being aware of it, what Heidegger called the ready-at-handedness of things, that they are *always already* classified as something, before we start to think or speak about them. In this way, language is biased towards essentialism. One advantage of conceptual modelling is that it remains neutral on this point. If there are essences, they will have to be discovered empirically, and not be imported through the structure of language.

13. States of mind

I have so far considered the structure of conceptual thinking and the targets of conceptual thinking. There is one further component to this system, which is subject of cognition, the thinking being that is the location of the actualisation and application of conceptual entities. Ontologically, a subject of cognizance is an actualised entity whose states, including its states of mind, evolve through a sequence of events. Because the subject of cognition is also an object of cognition, it is able to inhabit a unique state, that of self-awareness.

The state of a subject of cognizance has a number of different levels. Firstly, there are the epistemological states: those of knowing, believing, assuming, doubting, concluding and so on. Secondly, there are the set of emotional states: the states of wellbeing or malaise, calm, turbulence and distraction, self-confidence, worry and anxiety. Thirdly, there are the set of attitudes: benevolence or malevolence, anger and indignation at injustice, compassion for suffering and so on.

Each of these sets of states is likely to be both a cause and an effect. Attitudes tend to be expressed in emotional states. What makes the distinction worth drawing is that attitudes are represented in the mind, whereas emotional states are the means of representing in the mind physical and biological states. For example, the attitude of indignation has an objective correlative (to borrow T.S. Eliot's phrase) in the observation of injustice towards others. In his book *The Strange Order of Things*, Antonio Damasio argues that our emotional states are the way in which the state of our being is represented in the mind.

We don't have a cognitive representation of the state of our being, but the information is communicated as an emotional state.

That means that emotions and attitudes may drift apart. The distinction usually drawn between fear and anxiety is that fear has an object, a thing or event to be feared, whereas anxiety is a state without a focus. While the source of fear can be dealt with, an anxious person can't identify the source of their anxiety and thereby apply a corrective course of action. Similarly, anger may not have an object, and if you don't know what you are angry at, you may be angry at everything.

One advantage of thinking about the subject of cognizance in this way, as a component of the organism whose purpose includes surveillance of the functioning of that whole entity in its surroundings and subsequent co-ordination of a response to that environment with the purpose of maintaining a steady state, is that we can avoid falling into the error of thinking that cognitive sub-systems are somehow separate from the functioning of the other sub-systems in an organism – Descartes's error, as Damasio calls it.

Cartesian dualism was a product of the Scientific Revolution. In the Aristotelian system, living organisms were a subset of physical entities, and human beings a subset of living organisms. The capacity to think wasn't any more problematic than the capacity to move, to grow and to reproduce. However, in the way Descartes interpreted the new sciences, physical structures have existence, duration and extent, whereas intellectual structures have existence and duration but not extent.

The principal division between things, which in Aristotelian thinking had been between physical objects and living organisms, shifted to the distinction between human minds and everything else. The same transition meant that minds became purely the subjects of cognition, and epistemology tended to displace ontology and logic as the central discipline in philosophical thinking.

The legacy of this move is the mind-body problem, the central problem in the philosophy of mind and probably in modern philosophy. This outcome is odd in some ways, since the mechanical model of physics was superseded in the 18th century and none of Descartes's successors followed his thinking.

What underlies the modern version of the mind-body problem is the assumption of causal closure, although this is rarely declared explicitly. The causal closure argument is that natural science more generally and physics more particularly can explain everything. It is an argument that conflates description with explanation. If every system is a physical system, then it can be described in physical terms, but the claim that physics explains everything requires resources from ontology, epistemology, and logic, and in that sense is defeated before it begins.

This account of the way we think leads to a kind of fallibilism rather than skepticism as such. It's not that we can't know anything, but discovery is difficult and error prone, and we don't fully understand how the tools we use work. There are three components that go towards the construction of fallibilism: the fallible mind, the limitations of the conceptual tools and techniques available, and what might be called the opacity of the real world.

Firstly, there are the limitations of the human mind that have been investigated by cognitive science: over-confidence, a tendency to jump to conclusions and an unwillingness to follow the evidence, a failure to be cognizant of the ambiguities and errors of perception, introspection, and memory. In contemporary debates, we often have on the one side a scientific and technological over-confidence and, on the other, the certainties of intuition and testimony that underpin, in so many cases, religious thinking.

Secondly, there are the limitations of the tools and techniques available, the limitations not just of conceptual thinking, but also of intuitive and imaginative thinking; more broadly the limitations of logic and epistemology. The perspectival nature of experience and thinking means that the objective point-of-view has to be constructed. And, just like any other construction, that takes time, cooperation and co-ordination, and trial and error.

Thirdly, there is the opacity of the real world. This is the idea that reality cannot be taken at face value. It doesn't carry its structure, function and dynamics on the surface, these things have to be excavated. Our experience is inherently noisy. There is no particular relation between the mind and the world which will allow it to bypass its limitations or the limitations of its methods, tools and techniques.

The contrary belief is what I have been calling the bias to believe. Under this assumption, the burden of proof, so to speak, is placed on the sceptic; the default position being to take things at face value. Because so much of our thinking is intuitive, this view carries with it the idea of intuition as reliable knowledge.

It is an idea that has a long history. It is inherent in the idea of the *vita contemplativa*, the ideal of knowledge as something acquired by stilling the activity of the mind. It is also present in much religious and mystical thinking. My feeling is that what the Roman Catholic church opposes as relativism is really opposition to fallibilism. If personal experience and testimony are fallible, is there a reliable foundation for faith? The bias to believe often accompanies the idea that there is a reality beyond or below the appearance of the world with which the mind has an affinity and which it can know intuitively because in some way it is identified with it.

This isn't just a critique of intuitive thinking. Scientific and technological confidence is often grounded in what Erwin Schrödinger called the hypothesis of the understandability of nature: the idea that, in principle at least, a complete and unequivocal understanding of nature is a realistic objective for science.

These look like different versions of the same error. I think that Daniel Kahneman is right in this regard and that the reach for certainty is a weakness of the fallible mind. For this reason, rationality can't simply be taken as a means to counter ignorance, prejudice and superstition. It has to be also critical and reflexive and conscious of its own limitations if it isn't to fall into the same trap of over-confident assertion.

In the introduction I proposed that a broadly empirical epistemology is one that recognises that cognition is fallible and corrigible. Knowledge has traditionally been taken to be not just a state of alignment between representation and what is represented, but also the presence of sufficient evidence to support the representation. To be knowledge, beliefs need not only to be true but also to be justified. This level of confidence falls short of the certainty that is implicit in a claim to knowledge.

In everyday speech, we distinguish knowledge from belief or opinion. Typically, we might say we *know* if we have first-hand experience, and we *believe* or *have an opinion* if our information comes from the testimony of others. Similarly, if we have reviewed a document, run an experiment or carried out a computation ourselves, rather than basing our view on the testimony of others, we might claim that we know something as opposed to believing it. Even then, we might not treat first-hand experience as entirely reliable. Perhaps we were there, but visibility was poor, the event at a distance, we were distracted. Perhaps we carried out the computation, but the calculation is complicated and difficult and it's easy to make mistakes. The other reason we might say that we know something is that the process through which it was determined is reliable. This is the basis of confidence in scientific knowledge. The scientific method is designed to mitigate these problems.

Both knowing and believing are states of the mind that are concerned not so much with the mapping between model and target but with our ability to assess accurately the level to which this mapping applies. Rather than just knowledge and belief, our cognitive states could be categorised on a graduated scale. On such a scale, we might have, at one end, beliefs that are proven and, at the other, beliefs that are untenable; and then, between these, a graduated scale of degrees of tenability, plausibility and justification.

Here, what criteria are applied and where the division between categories lies is less important than the idea of a graduated scale. However, my suggestion would be the criteria that have already been discussed: scope, simplicity, coherence, consistency, adequacy, the absence of arbitrariness, necessity, and the level of appropriate confirmatory evidence.

On such a scale, a belief might be untenable if it contradicted a justified or proven belief, or if it was incoherent or inconsistent, the state of being *not even wrong*, in Wolfgang Pauli's well-known put-down. Plausibility might require, in addition to coherence and consistency, a level of explanatory adequacy regarding the question being asked and some level of confirmatory evidence. There would be many degrees of plausibility.

There would also be many degrees of justifiability. Justifiability implies a higher standard than mere plausibility; application to a wide class of observations, simplicity, coherence, consistency, adequacy to the question being asked, the minimum of arbitrary elements; necessity; supported by a substantial body of confirmatory evidence from multiple perspectives, and so on.

The final category, proven beliefs, would be relatively small and likely restricted to formal disciplines such as logic and mathematics. When used elsewhere, in a law court for example, there tends always to be rider, such as proven *beyond reasonable doubt*.

Scientific theories often start out as plausible conjectures. Some even as implausible conjectures. A good example is continental drift, which was first proposed by Alfred Wegener in the 1920s, to answer some questions about observations of the flora and fauna of different regions, but which seemed implausible to many in the field because there was no apparent mechanism. Only later, with the understanding of plate tectonics, and the idea that one tectonic plate can descend below another when they converge, did the theory move from implausible to plausible, and then, through the continued accumulation of evidence and integration with other theories such as evolution, become a justified theory.

This does raise a question about what it means to have rational belief. At one time it would have been rational but mistaken to find the theory of continental drift implausible, and intuitive but correct to give the theory credence. The lesson I draw from this is that calibrating belief is not just a question of looking at conjectures and evidence now, but considering the envelope of possibilities and the overall state of information. In that sense, sets of beliefs are analogous to living documents, they are undergoing a continual process of evolution.

So, we don't really believe the scientific image of the world as it now stands. Nor do we not believe it. Rather, current theory is the best supported theory that we have. If the theory changes, as it did in the case of plate tectonics, we don't lose confidence in the scientific method. We expect theories to change.

This is the main difference between critical thinking and intuitive thinking. It would be odd to insist that you are confident in today's intuitions, and at the same time that you were equally confident in yesterday's intuitions, though they turned out to be mistaken. The proper lesson to draw would be that intuitions are fallible.

IV. INTERIORITY

14. Subjectivity and interiority

The argument of this essay is that reflective intelligence is the outcome of the co-location of interiority and conceptualisation. This co-location is contingent, in the sense that it might never have happened, but also a contingent necessity, because one cannot be actualised without the other; you either get both or neither. Once you have an incipient interiority, you are likely to get the actualisation of concepts, because conceptualisation, having no state, is always already there. The load-bearing idea is that only beings of a specific kind placed in a specific predicament can be reflectively intelligent, but that reflective intelligence isn't a product of nature, because concepts are not a product of nature.

The structure of this chapter is a chain of arguments. This first section connects subjectivity to interiority and interiority to rationality. The second section covers the different types of reasoning; the third the decision-making that connects reasoning to the initiation of actions; and the fourth the types of actions that can be initiated. Then, in the final two sections, I consider the types and the location, the *where*, of agency and the related concepts of personal autonomy and personal freedom.

The characteristic feature of the human condition is its interiority or inwardness. While conscious awareness and subjectivity are shared with other minds, self-awareness is a marker of human exceptionalism, along with language, conceptualisation and a capacity to reason. As a package, this can be called sapience.

Interiority doesn't arrive on the scene fully formed. It is a product of evolution from individuation by way of subjectivity. If we can find the origins of biology in individuation, subjectivity in biology, and interiority in subjectivity, we can bridge the gaps and create a continuity between these different states.

Interiority has a number of layers. Firstly, there is the interiority that flows from physical existence and is inherited from the individuation of entities and events that characterises everything there is. Secondly, there is the interiority that flows from subjectivity, and the resulting point-of-view and agenda, that are the consequence of the evolution of life. Thirdly, there is the interiority that flows from the structuring of events in time, the nature of practical reasoning, the inevitable weaving of courses of action into the wider course of events and the unavoidable jeopardy that flows from these. And, finally, there is the fourth layer, the interiority that flows from being brought up and educated in a particular cultural, economic, social, political and technological environment, all outcomes of the processes of cultural acquisition.

The central question in most modern philosophical thinking is the distinction between the mental and the physical. This is because arguments typically start from the premise that there are physical entities and events and mental entities and events, and we have to find some way of bridging the gap between them, or reducing one to the other. This assumption seems to me to be unnecessarily question begging.

The alternative premise is usually called neutral monism. This is the idea that to begin the investigation by dividing the world up into physical and mental components is premature – we should only do that if we find a reason to.

There are three steps to the argument. Firstly, the path from subjectivity to interiority is an evolution, not a radical break. Secondly, introspection and conceptual rationality are a package, such that you can have both or neither, but not one without the other. The third part of the argument is that interiority and conceptual rationality are the basis of personal autonomy in practical reasoning, judgement and decision-making.

The basic premise is that interiority is a mode of subjectivity, subjectivity is a mode of life and life a mode of individuation. Individuation is the basic characteristic of all entities. It is the necessary but not sufficient condition of all other modes of existence. In this analysis, there are three principal break points: firstly, the division between, on the one hand, physical systems and structures, and, on the other, living organisms; secondly, the division within living organisms between non-sentient organisms and sentient beings; and, thirdly, the division within sentient beings between the consciously aware and the introspectively self-aware.

Less abstractly, these divisions are marked by the distinction between living organisms and other natural structures and systems, the distinction between animals and other living organisms, and the distinction between human beings and animals.

Living organisms differ from other natural structures and systems to the degree to which they are adapted to ensure their own survival and reproduction. There is no mechanism that sustains a river system, holding it together, in the way that there is with a living organism. Not all living organisms are sentient. Plants are also individuated, and share with animals the characteristics of living organisms, but a plant has no subjectivity because it doesn't have any of the centralised systems to track and respond to the environment and therefore it doesn't need a central system for co-ordination and control.

In animals, there is not only a distribution of function but a centralised surveillance capability, implemented as the neural system, to monitor the way in which the organism is functioning, co-ordinate information about its state and environment, and communicate adjustments to the appropriate component in order to maintain the homeostatic functioning of the whole.

Sentience will generate a point-of-view and agenda, and these are the basic attributes of subjectivity. For this exposition, I have drawn on the work of Peter Godfrey-Smith, and in particular his essay, *Materialism, Subjectivity, and Evolution*, which argues that while our ability to build a picture of the evolutionary origins of subjectivity is still quite limited, an outline appears to be possible. He identifies point-of-view and agenda as the basic components of subjectivity and sketches a picture of their biological evolution.

> *A picture we might start out from recognizes two concepts: subjectivity and agency. These have different emphases – subjectivity is more a matter of the input side; agency involves the output side. But from a biological point of view and perhaps others, these are largely correlative and complementary capacities; sensing and action coevolved, and each gives the other its point. Initially, I'll think of subjects as having a pair of features: (i) a point of view on the world, and (ii) an agenda. Subjects act in ways that reflect both.*

That is, what distinguishes subjects is subjectivity; subjective experience is the experience of a subject. In Thomas Nagel's formulation, there is a *something it's like to be* about subjective experience. The model is in the form of a process with inputs and outputs. The inputs are sensory perception constrained by point-of-view and the outputs are the feel for and evaluation of experience.

Even the simplest prokaryotic organisms, such as bacteria, have the capacity to detect changes in their environment and co-ordinate their movement in response. Multi-cellular systems in animals have more evolved capabilities; in particular, sensory structures such as eyes that make it possible to track the environment at a macro-scale, systems of muscles that allow co-ordinated movement in response, and nervous systems that function as control systems to link the two together.

Nervous systems are present in corals, jellyfish and anemones as well as in animals with bilateral body plans. This was an evolutionary divergence that occurred over 600 million years ago in the Ediacaran period, indicating that these systems appeared very early in the evolution of life on Earth.

In the Cambrian period, which began around 540 million years ago, more sophisticated sensory and motor systems evolved and animals started to interact with each other. These interactions often took the form of predation. Godfrey-Smith notes that the pre-Cambrian world was probably quite a peaceful one.

Animals in three groups have since developed complex active bodies capable of rapid motion, the ability to sense at a distance and the capacity to manipulate objects. These three groups are the cephalopods, the arthropods and the vertebrates. The cephalopods are the marine molluscs: octopus, squid and cuttlefish; the arthropods include both marine dwellers such as crabs and land dwellers such as insects and spiders; and the vertebrates are the fish, amphibians, reptiles, birds and mammals.

Connectedly, these forms are also characterised by image-forming eyes, the capacity to integrate sensory information, the ability to track the effects of the animal's own actions on what it senses (an ability called *compensation for reafference*), and instrumental learning.

Image-forming eyes support a genuine view of macro-scale objects. The integration of diverse sensory channels generates the subjective point-of-view. Compensation for reafference indicates the beginnings of a distinction between self and other; and, finally, instrumental learning supports the capacity of an animal to track the link between its actions and their positive or negative consequences, and to adapt its behaviour accordingly. It is through instrumental learning that an animal's agenda is brought within internal control.

Intuitively, we might think that increasing sophistication on the input and the output side would go together, but Godfrey-Smith suggests that this isn't always the case. Insects may be more evolved on the sensory side, especially those that can fly, but they typically live very short, very routine lives. This makes sense if the adult stage of an insect's life is lived as little more than a disposable reproduction machine.

On the other hand, although molluscs such as slugs and snails have much more limited sensory capabilities, there is some evidence to suggest that they are capable of instrumental learning. In seasnails, for example, a damaging event appears to lead to a state of negative readiness in the organism, a kind of corporeal wariness or vigilance. Such a capacity would make sense in an animal such as a seasnail that is vulnerable to damage but is also relatively long-lived and has the ability to repair itself.

This kind of differentiation is relevant to the question of whether the evolution of subjectivity in living organisms is gradual or organised around thresholds. Does subjective experience arise gradually, along a smooth gradient; or does it arise instantaneously with the crossing of some threshold? The threshold model holds that there is some minimal level of complexity which must be reached in order to generate subjectivity. A question this then poses is: what features suffice for an animal to be sentient? The gradualist model, on the other hand, tries to account for how some organisms have internal workings that are experiential.

Godfrey-Smith notes that in this domain much is tentative, but the gradualist model is supported by the distribution of features among living organisms and the existence of every possible intermediate and partial case, both on the sensory side and the evaluation side. It seems, for example, there may be some level of reafference compensation, and therefore the glimmer of a sense of self, even in nematode worms.

Godfrey-Smith is describing biological features that start to close the apparent gap between the body and the mind. These features are not just kinds of complexity. They give an entity a point-of-view, create a sense of self versus others, and endow events with a positive or negative value. Once we have subjects, we have subjectivity.

> The idea is that with a filled-out story of this kind – one that I have only sketched here, but which I think we can glimpse – there is no extra question of whether there's something it's like to be an animal of these sort. Once we have subjects, subjectivity comes along. The way it feels to be a system of this kind comes along.

The idea is that once you have animals, which are individual entities of a certain kind, then point-of-view and agenda inevitably follow, there is no need to invoke something else in order to complete the explanation.

If we accept that subjectivity is an evolutionary product, can we also accept that introspection is one? The development of specifically human capabilities such as the use of language and the ability to understand conceptual meaning requires evolution beyond subjectivity, but what the account of the evolution of subjectivity suggests is that this subsequent evolution from subjectivity to interiority is incremental. It has much less to achieve than might be supposed, because most of the work has been done in getting to subjectivity.

For example, this subsequent evolution doesn't have to establish macro-scale imaging of the environment, it doesn't have to generate a point-of-view or separate the self from the environment, and it doesn't have to learn how to learn. These features and capabilities are all inherited from the evolution of sentient beings. The continuity can be seen as evidence that language, conceptual thinking and rationality can evolve in sentient beings in the same way that subjectivity can evolve in living organisms. The narrower the gap, the more plausible is the possibility that it can and has been bridged.

The progression from individuation to introspection by way of life and subjectivity is a series of incremental changes in the modality of existence. There is thus no special difficulty in locating introspective and conceptual rationality in the scientific image of the world. A gradualist analysis can be applied both to the evolution of subjectivity and the evolution of introspection. This means that there is no need to put forward a reductionist explanation that seeks to understand rational, cultural, and social events as physical, chemical, and biological events. Just as the difference between sentient and non-sentient living organisms represents both a difference and continuity, the distinction between subjectivity and interiority isn't a different difference, as it were, that requires some special form of explanation. It is highly likely that a future biological science will be able to explain how these discontinuities were crossed, developing the filled-out story that Godfrey-Smith refers to.

However, at the same time, there are no grounds for supposing that it isn't a real difference. In the case of a human beings, the mode of individuation is self-conscious rationality. We are aware of our own individuation. As Antonio Damasio puts it in his book *The Strange Order of Things*:

> In normal circumstances, when we are awake and alert, without fuss or deliberation, the images that flow in the mind have a perspective – ours. We spontaneously recognise ourselves as the subjects of mental experiences...we each appreciate mental contents in a distinct perspective, mine or yours...

> The term "consciousness" applies to the very natural but distinctive kind of mental state described by the above traits. That mental state allows its owner to be the private experiencer of the world around and, just as important, to experience aspects of his or her own being...

> It is tempting to simply talk about "subjectivity" and leave behind the term "consciousness" and the distractions it tends to cause. We should resist the temptation, because the term "consciousness" conveys an additional and important component of conscious

states: integrated experience, which consists of placing mental contents into a more or less unified multidimensional panorama.

As this passage makes clear, in this domain terms often lack agreed meanings, and Damasio means by consciousness what I have been calling the self-awareness that is the distinctive feature of interiority. However, it seems odd to me to say that an octopus or a dolphin lacks consciousness, and for that reason I prefer the terms subjectivity and interiority. Subjectivity is what separates animals from other living organisms, while interiority is what separates human beings from other animals. My view is that it is more intuitive to think of animals as conscious beings with integrated experience while at the same time recognising the basis of human exceptionalism in the capacity for introspection or self-consciousness.

Introspective awareness creates the platform for language, cultural acquisition and cultural transmission. As Damasio continues:

In conclusion, subjectivity and integrated experience are the critical components of consciousness...subjectivity and consciousness are essential enablers of the cultural mind. In the absence of subjectivity, nothing matters; in the absence of some degree of integrated experience, the reflection and discernment that are required for creativity are not possible.

The picture of the diachronic identity of persons that emerges from this analysis emphasises both the continuity and the discontinuity between the individuation of human beings, the individuation of animals and the individuation of systems and structures more generally.

This implies that human beings have multiple bases for identity through time, not just continuity in the sense of self, but also the continuity that comes from being sentient, from being a living organism and ultimately from being an individuated entity. Human beings are different, but not that different. Introspective beings inherit identity through time from individuation and point-of-view and agenda from subjectivity. In this way, personal identity is built up in layers.

One question this raises is how this layering works. One model would see these layers as discrete, so that, rather like oil floating on water, interiority is a capacity that floats on top of subjectivity which in turn floats on top of life. The other model, which is the one that I favour, is that these are different modes of functioning, that subjectivity is a mode of living, rather than an add-on, and that interiority is another mode of living.

There is therefore no need to ground personal identity in the continuity of consciousness. Personal identity through time is already given by the time there are introspectively aware beings. The individuality of human beings isn't fundamental; rather, what is fundamental is individuation, and the individuation generates individuality. The individuality of human beings flows from the deeper layers of individuation.

However, diversity of type and variation within type will tend to flow naturally from individuation. We are different because we are self-consciously aware of ourselves as individuals and therefore of the openness of the paths available to us. The scope for innovation and improvisation that comes from reflective awareness will tend to generate individuality. The full possibilities of individuality can be actualised only with the more sophisticated functions that come firstly with subjectivity and, even more powerfully, from introspection – that is, from the interiority that characterises self-aware beings. The identity through time that flows from individuation turns into the unity of the self, and the diversity and variety of individual existence into a self-aware individuality.

We live not only in a particular place, but also at a particular moment in cultural, intellectual, social, economic and political evolution. We are also tied to a human existence, and therefore a linear sequence of events in time. For this reason, interiority limits and defines and, hence, personal autonomy and freedom might be thought to require some means of escaping these limitations. My view is that this isn't necessary; instead, interiority provides the basis of personal autonomy and the possibility, though often not the reality, of personal freedom.

The solution to this paradox lies in the multiplicity of layers that make up the conditions of life. These could be defined in different ways; it's the idea of layering that is essential in this model. I suggest the following five layers: the stream of experience; internal representation; conceptualisation; discourses and disciplines; and, finally, critical reflection. The stream of experience and its representations are primarily functions of the mind as a natural entity. The structuring of intellectual discourses and disciplines and reflective critical thinking are primarily outcomes of the historical evolution of conceptual thinking. Conceptualisation is where the join is created, where experience and representation becomes reflective.

We don't undergo a sequence of experiences; rather, experiences update an inner representation. As experience accumulates through life, the relationship between specific experience and our accumulated internal representation becomes more and more unequal. At the same time, we acquire intellectual sophistication and the capacity for critical reflection. In this way our conceptual thinking is augmented from both ends.

It is a consequence of this layering that the integrated point-of-view of subjectivity is overcome. These layers don't represent a single structure; they are multiple standpoints from which events can be viewed. We can say that, as a consequence of self-awareness, we don't have a single point-of-view and agenda, we have multiple points-of-view and multiple agendas, and these must adjust, adapt, and accommodate each other in order to arrive at not only a reasonable intellectual unity but also a reasonable psychological unity. One side-effect of this process is that we see one part of ourselves from another part. We can view both our experience and representations from the perspective of our critical thinking, and our critical thinking from the perspective of our experience and representations.

Interiority implies situatedness, but, at the same time, it supports rationality and rationality serves to mitigate the situatedness. The self can be detached not only from its experience, but from its own representations, and cultural and intellectual acquisition. There is an elusive self as much as a situated self, and it is this elusiveness that is the basis of personal autonomy, and where social, cultural and political evolution has been sufficient, the basis of actual freedom. It is this that brings complexity to instrumentality, timeliness and jeopardy, the component features of agency.

This means that human beings aren't just more intelligent animals with better solutions to the problems posed by subjectivity, but beings situated in a very specific predicament, a predicament generated by rationality and introspection. This generates the uncertainty of action, the necessity of choice, the possibility of absurdity, and the awareness of mortality.

The narrowness of the gap between subjectivity and introspection isn't an indicator of how difficult it is to cross. We could ask, why did it take so long for interiority to evolve? On the other hand, we don't know what a reasonable span of time might be, since we have only the one data point for evidence, human evolution. We don't know how prevalent life, let alone subjectivity and interiority, is in the universe. I like to think we may one day be able to answer such questions.

The narrowness of the gap is also not an indicator of the scope that opens up once the gap is bridged. This depends on the territory that the bridge gives access to. In the remaining sections, I will cover some aspects of this terrain: the different types of reasoning, the different types of action, and the ethical and political questions that these give rise to.

15. Theoretical and practical reasoning

There is a relatively straightforward connection between interiority and practical reasoning. The situatedness that comes from interiority is the background condition to instrumental reasoning. A point-of-view and agenda generate value, the sense that things matter. Jeopardy follows, from the possibility both that things may go awry or opportunities may be missed, and potential value lost.

The term *theory* comes from the same Greek root as the term *theatre*, and conveys an idea of spectatorship, a kind of detachment from what is being observed. The goal of theoretical reasoning is explanation and understanding. It seeks to understand entities and events: how systems are constituted and how they evolve through time. It is concerned with the construction and application of conceptual models; the relationship between hypothesis and evidence; the requirements of confirmation; and the calibration of the level of support that confirmatory evidence gives to hypotheses. The goal is a conceptual model that is adequate to the domain of application.

Theorising is characterised by abstraction and generality. Conceptual models are abstract structures which can be applied to many target objects and the objective is to achieve an appropriate degree of generality. A complex model might apply to a complex target and a simple model to a simple target, but what we are usually looking for are the models that have an extensive domain of application that is achieved with an economy of means.

Theoretical explanation therefore tends to generalisations about types of entities and events. Because theory is the mind engaged in the construction and application of conceptual models, it is drawn to ignore the specificities of the individual entity or event in favour of what is common to the class. This tendency to abstraction and generalisation holds also for the point-of-view from which the explanation is offered and the audience towards which it is directed. Theoretical explanations are meant to be neutral, applying from every possible point-of-view and meaningful to every possible audience.

Theorising is therefore characterised by exteriority. A theorist tries to escape their specific standpoint in order to find an understanding that is independent of any particular perspective. The issue here is not that perspective necessarily generates error, but that it is partial. It is not possible to escape perspective – there is no Archimedean standpoint as such – but one can be synthesised by aggregating and reconciling multiple standpoints, eliminating contradictions and incoherencies, and closing gaps, in order to arrive at a result that approximates a non-perspectival understanding. The actual degree of objectivity attained by the resulting understanding will be a function of how comprehensive is the set of input points-of-view, and how skilfully they have been aggregated.

Theoretical reasoning has a formal component concerned with conceptual modelling and an evidentiary component concerned with application and confirmation. It is the second which makes theory backward looking. We understand and explain looking backwards because the evidence that confirms a theory must be something that is happening or has already happened.

This doesn't mean that the future is not important to theory. The ability to predict how things will go is an important test of whether the system has been understood. Theorists try to understand how types of system function and evolve by building and testing conceptual models. The models are constructed on the basis of what is already known, and tested by using them to make predictions about a future that can be confirmed.

A great deal of theorising is now carried out within the framework of specialised disciplines in the humanities and the sciences. This division of labour has huge advantages in terms of the development of the arts and sciences, but professionalisation and specialisation also has its disadvantages. For one thing, the institutionalisation of knowledge brings with it an inevitable bureaucracy and an inevitable politicisation. It also poses an impediment to synthesis between specialist fields; and a fracture between specialist domains and the general culture. The disciplines of the humanities and the sciences as forms of critical thinking are constrained by the scope of the specialism. The flipside of disciplinary autonomy is that explanation stops at the frontier. In a highly specialised environment, conceptual theorising can tend to become a set of technical accomplishments, rather than a world-view. For this reason, this specialisation adds an additional set of obstacles to the possibility of an integrated understanding of the world.

Where theoretical reasoning is characterised by generality, practical reasoning is characterised by singularity. Practical reasoning requires both an agent and an agenda. It is the reasoning of an agent determining a particular course of action in a particular set of circumstances. Like theoretical reasoning, it is concerned with conceptual models, hypotheses and evidence, but these are focused on a specific situation. The test of success is lucidity; the objective is a lucid understanding of the predicament and an adequate response to it in a course of action.

Explanation in practical thinking also pays as much attention to singularity and difference than generality and commonality, and therefore tends towards the concrete and the specific. It is concerned with the totality of a particular situation and how that situation might evolve. The reason for this is that theory is concerned with classes, and classes are formed by looking for what is common. Practical reasoning cannot draw this distinction in the same way; the significant detail may be somewhere in the singularity of the situation rather than the commonality. Practical reasoning must focus much more attentively on the totality of a situation. It must be as much concerned with individuality as typicality.

The specificity of practical reasoning originates in and is closely tied to the individuation of entities and events. Individuation carries with it a specific location in space and time and therefore a set of specific relationships to everything else. There is not just the individuation of the agent, but also the individuation of every participant and bystander and every object.

A practical explanation is offered from an engaged point-of-view and intended for an engaged and interested audience. It is, like conceptual theorising, concerned with the world, but from the perspective of a particular agent in a particular situation. Practical deliberation is a time-dependent engagement with a worldly predicament. The outcome of practical reasoning is a decision to initiate a course of action here and now that can be defended and explained. Its substance is shaped by this context.

This doesn't preclude the possibility that practical reasoning may be hypothetical, a sort of dry run or trial of ideas of what we might do were we in a particular predicament, in order to be better prepared and to arrive at a clearer idea of the basic principles involved. But such hypothetical reasoning lacks the jeopardy that initiating an actual course of action supplies.

Borges called one of his stories *The garden of forking paths* and this is a good description of the human predicament. We can't go back, we can't stop, and we can't step off the path. There is always a decision to be made in the here and now. While the future paths are open-ended and undetermined, the choice at each junction changes the pattern of future possible paths, shutting down some, changing the probabilities of others. Every course of action is in this sense a projection into the future. This is the consequence of interiority and is the reason why a human life cannot be lived from the outside.

The outcome of practical thinking is a decision to undertake a course of action; effectively, it is a decision to occupy a passage of time in a particular way, and it is the passage of time that conditions the character of practical thinking. A course of action is initiated, then sustained, or perhaps endured, and then brought to a close. A period of time is occupied. Because the passage of time is a defining feature of action, it is also a defining feature of practical reasoning. The period of time will happen anyway, and will be occupied by some course of action, but only one course of action is possible, and what is to be decided is which specific course of action will occupy a particular passage of time.

Jeopardy is a consequence of interiority, and the fact that a course of action occupies an amount of time and time is finite for every individuated entity. It a consequence of the occupation of time. There are two aspects to this. The first is the harm that will flow from poor choices; the second the possibility of opportunities missed. The balance between avoiding harm and missing opportunity is an underlying and unresolvable tension.

Practical reasoning is the form of reasoning which answers the question: how are we going to occupy this passage of time in conditions of jeopardy? The passage of time is also the foundation for instrumental reasoning. Instrumental rationality is a component of practical reasoning.

Very abstractly, instrumental reasoning is a process of mapping the current state of a system to possible future states based on a knowledge of how the components of a system or structure behave, how the system or structure might evolve, and how it might be possible to intervene to steer the evolution of the system or structure in a particular direction. It is the dimension of time that gives instrumental reasoning a purchase in practical reasoning. Instrumental reasoning is used to map the state of a system at the start of a passage of time to the desired state of the system at the end of the passage of time in order to identify possible interventions in the course of events in order to arrive at a particular future state or to guide the evolution of a system along a particular path.

In this respect, instrumental reasoning is also a form of theoretical reasoning. It is neutral with regard to what the end-state should be. Instrumental reasoning isn't in itself sufficient to come to a decision regarding a course of action because it doesn't include the reasoning which decides what the purpose of the course of action should be – why this period of time is to be occupied in this way. In other words, instrumental reasoning doesn't supply the evaluations that drive practical reasoning. Practical reasoning draws on theory and instrumentality, but these are not sufficient in themselves to drive practical reasoning.

The dichotomy of theory and practice should be distinguished from two similar and related but different antitheses. One is the antithesis between subjective and objective. What we mean by objectivity is that what is being thought and said is about the object; it contains nothing about the observer, the subject of cognizance. In reality it's not possible to observe something without the presence of an observer, so in practice, objectivity implies observer-neutrality. An objective conceptual understanding will be the same for all observers and therefore independent of any observer. It is the view from anywhere, which is also the view from nowhere.

Furthermore, the relationship between conceptual model and target is not something that exists in nature. There must be an observer, a theorist, to apply one to the other. For this reason, the theoretical perspective is a kind of imagined place-to-stand. In this sense the view from the outside is a construction built through the processes and procedures of an intellectual discipline. It is arrived at by identifying and eliminating what belongs to multiple subjective projections.

Subjectivity, on the other hand, means related to the subject of cognizance. The meaning of the object remains the same, but the significance is relative to the point-of-view and motivations of the observer. The subject–object distinction is frequently regarded as a dichotomy, but to this way of thinking subjective judgements supply something additional to objective judgements, and therefore remain complementary to objectivity, not in conflict with it.

Since the outside view is an imaginary standpoint which cannot actually be occupied, it has to be synthesised through the aggregation of many singular points-of-view. This connects the subject–object distinction to a second related antithesis, the public–private distinction. Since it is a synthesis, the objective view is also usually a public construction. It has a kind of transparency. Objectivity and publicity are interconnected.

This can tend to the view that personal testimony of private experience can't be part of public discussion because it cannot be subject to public confirmation. This is true in the direct sense, but testimony about private experience can still be evaluated. Testimony can always be examined: how many witnesses are there, what is their credibility, under what conditions were the observations made, is there counter-testimony, and so on.

The motivations and grounding for practical deliberation are often opaque and based on inside information and private intentions. However, it is not essential to practical reasoning that it should be opaque from the outside. Practical reasoning is public reasoning when it becomes the reasoning of an institutional entity. Deliberative assemblies of one kind or another – councils, corporations, courts and parliaments – are all engaged in public practical reasoning.

The distinction between the transparent and the opaque doesn't align with the distinction between practical and theoretical. Practical reasoning would not turn into theoretical reasoning if it were conducted entirely in public. The interiority of practical reasoning isn't privacy so much as it is reasoning from the inside of a predicament and living inside the course of action that is the outcome of practical decision-making.

In summary, although it has different objectives and structures, theoretical reasoning can play a role in practical reasoning. Value and instrumentality distinguish practical reasoning from theoretical reasoning, and both are linked to interiority. The detachment that comes from theoretical reasoning can be both a respite from the pressures of value and instrumentality and a means of expanding the horizon of practical thinking. Creativity and imagination can make a similar contribution. These different modes of thinking can be integrated in critical reflection.

16. Decision-making and critical reflection

Practical reasoning is a response to a predicament that has been brought about by a course of events, and the outcome of a course of practical reasoning is a decision to initiate a course of action – to launch it into the ongoing course of events in such a way as to change that course of events. It therefore involves the time-limited integration of the judgements and the decisions made in a constrained set of circumstances. Timeliness and value are salient attributes of these courses of action. Decisions are always made here and now, even when they are decisions about future actions, and they always have value, they matter. It is this combination of value and situatedness in time that creates the jeopardy that is central to practical reasoning.

There are a number of phases to the process of deliberation and decision-making, among them diagnosis, simplification, prioritisation, explanation and justification. They don't always happen in this sequence. Ordinarily you would expect to work forward from a diagnosis to explanation and justification, but the process may not always be linear. It can jump about and cycle round, and there will be cases where the most important feature of the outcome is not that it is the solution to a problem but that it is explicable and will seem justified to a particular audience.

Decision-making is firstly grounded in diagnostics. This involves identifying a particular predicament as an instance of a class or type. The term *diagnosis* originated in medicine but it can be applied more generally. Through this identification a link can be made between possible causes for a state of affairs, the way in which the course of events might be expected to develop and the range of possible interventions that might be made to steer the evolution of the situation in a particular direction.

Within a particular field, diagnosis is a relatively contained, unambiguous and structured process. Even so, the underlying condition may not be obvious or unambiguous, and the prognosis, the way in which the situation will develop, can be unclear. Outside specialist domains, and their codifications, diagnosis is likely to be more open-ended, ambiguous and inconclusive. Interpretation is often rough and ready, the boundary between deliberative and intuitive reasoning is not always apparent, and complexity and lack of time militate against extensive investigation. A heuristic approach is often required to manage the complexity.

Moving from deliberation to decision-making typically involves processes of simplification and prioritisation. There are a number of common methods of simplifying decision-making. One is to take an evolutionary approach. To make things easier we typically repeat what we did the last time we faced a similar situation, with variations only at the margins, rather than re-evaluating everything from the ground up each time. Another simplification strategy is to partition our mental accounting rather than weighing every decision globally.

Furthermore, many decisions are made in the context of the roles we are engaged in and the situations in which that role is engaged. Decision-making can be simplified from being constrained by the structuring that comes from situations and roles. There are multiple roles that are associated with social networks, family structures, occupations and politics. Roles come with rights and duties, privileges and obligations, purposes and values. Particular roles are not necessarily imposed, but it's hard to be part of any society without engaging in at least a few.

If we have arrived at a set of possible courses of action, these have to be put into some kind of priority or order of preference. The most significant difficulty is that making choices is rarely a matter of comparing like with like. For example, there is always the need to balance the short term against the long term, the probable against the uncertain, and the safer against the riskier.

For that reason, deliberation isn't usually an algorithmic process of sorting a set of known options into an order of preference in the way proposed by axiomatic decision-making models such as rational choice theory and the expected utility hypothesis. The trade-offs required in decision-making have to be discovered and, in the process, the original preferences will come under review and may change. This obtains even more forcefully if the outcome has to be negotiated with other parties, when the real choices may be understood only in the course of bargaining.

Where deliberation, negotiation and decision-making are concerned with diagnosing situations and discovering preferences, justification in practical reasoning means advocacy, the forensic art of making a case. If the paradigm setting for diagnostics is medicine, the paradigm setting for advocacy is the law court. The diagnosis, the deliberation, the decision-making, the course of action undertaken and outcomes may all have to be explained and defended.

There is no rule that says that decisions have to be consistent. We are usually faced with multiple dynamics, scales and time-frames that require different and sometimes divergent responses. On the other hand, there is a rule that says that justifications ought to be consistent. An arbitrary and inconsistent justification would undermine itself and, in that sense, consistency can be said to be constitutive of justification.

Justification usually links decisions either to first principles or to outcomes, and often both. With regard to principles, the idea is that the case being considered falls under a principle as an instance of a general type, and it is by falling under the principle that sufficient justification for the course of action is obtained. So the logic is that the action is an instance of a type and the occurrences of the type have value. Something similar applies in the case of outcomes. In this case, the course of action is justified not by first principles, but rather the outcome. So the logic is that the course of action leads instrumentally to the outcome, and the outcome has value. These connections have different rationalities: the first by instance to type, the by second cause to effect. But in both cases the connection cannot be made arbitrarily. Arbitrary connections wouldn't serve this purpose.

Although justification is firstly aimed at ourselves, to give us confidence in our own decisions, there is usually also an external audience. The target audience is itself engaged in the course of events and, for that reason, advocacy is accountable to the current predicament and the parties engaged in it. Justifications are not usually addressed to a detached court.

The need to present a case to others will push us beyond the subjective point-of-view and the particular agenda while, at the same time, the same circumstances will limit the scope to what will be persuasive to the target audience. It may not always be possible to justify a course of action at the level of fine detail, however, and justifications sometimes have to be very abstract.

Justification often requires explanation. Explanation is similar to justification in that it is retrospective and is addressed both reflectively and to a wider audience. The difference between explanation and justification is one of purpose. Justification ultimately makes demands or appeals, where explanation provides insight and information. For that reason advocacy is often irksome and challenging, demanding some response from its audience, whether concurrence, rejection or indifference.

The explanatory mode is a means of creating a shared understanding, removing as far as possible misunderstanding, miscommunication, and misrepresentation. Theoretical explanations from the humanities and sciences inform the practical explanations of decision-making and their justifications. However, there is a no need for a presumption of concurrence or the idea that disagreement is evidence of a problem somewhere. Agreement is neither necessary nor always beneficial in practical reasoning. Diversity is the engine of disagreement but also necessary to knowledge and discovery. Accommodation and adaptation on the basis of an agreement to differ is usually sufficient. Premature or insincere agreement is a form of evasion.

Explanation is often absent in politics and public discourse. This is because the action of offering an explanation creates vulnerability, because explanations are corrigible. If an explanation is wrong, based on mistaken assumptions, misinformation or faulty reasoning, the course of action and the justifications offered to support it will be left hanging. A change of course will be necessary or the explanation will be exposed as a rationalisation or pretext rather than a genuine reason.

One question this raises is the degree to which justifications can be integrated with explanations. One potential consequence of the gap between theory and practice, if it turned out to be unbridgeable, is fragmentation and alienation. If we can't bring together what we do with what we believe, we will be left as strangers to our own lives, raising the problems of absurdity and futility. This concern with integration is specific to individuals. The gap between theory and practice is not a concern to the cosmos, so to speak; it only matters to critical reflective agents who are concerned with the integration of their actions and their beliefs.

Where conceptual theorising is pulled towards abstraction and detachment, practical deliberation is anchored in the concrete and engaged. Although the gap between theory and practice is a stubborn reality, there are methods of bridging it.

Firstly, instrumental rationality engages with both the neutrality of theoretical reasoning and the engagement of practical deliberation without integrating them. Secondly, critical reflection, which is more concrete than conceptual theorising and more detached than practical deliberation, narrows the gap sufficiently to allow for an integration of theory and practice, explanation and justification. Critical reflection is the location of this convergence because it is where concerns with the concrete and individuated meet with concerns with the abstract and general.

Reflective thinking is the mind looking at itself in the mirror; it is concerned with the questions: *What do I think I know, What do I believe, How do I feel, What do I want to achieve* and *What do I want to do with my time.* The end goal is a lucid understanding of oneself and one's predicament. Unlike practical thinking, it is concerned with what is the case rather than with what might be or should be the case. Unlike the theoretical disciplines of the humanities and sciences, it is concerned with the singular rather than the typical and with the integration of our point-of-view and agenda rather than the integration of our understanding of the target domain.

This means that critical reflection is concerned in the first instance with truthfulness. By this I mean that it is concerned with what we actually do believe rather than what we should believe, and what we actually want to do rather than what we should want to do. Questions of truth are not always resolvable, particularly in a timely fashion. Questions of truthfulness, because they are established by inward observation, can be.

Because it seeks to be truthful, reflective thinking can serve as a bridge between theory and practice. The simplest way of explaining this is to imagine that either side of the theoretical question *What should I believe* and the practical question *What should I do* there are a set of further questions. The question *What do I believe* naturally leads to two further questions *Why do I believe this* and *Am I right to believe it*, which is equivalent to *What should I believe*. In this way reflective thinking will be drawn naturally into conceptual theorising. Similarly, the question *What do I want to do* leads naturally to the questions *Why do I want to do this* and *Am I right to want to do it*, which again are equivalent to *What should I do*. Such a train of thought starts from the personal and the particular and ends in a view about what has value, what is worthwhile, more generally.

Reflection is innately private rather than public; publicity will tend to compromise the truthfulness that is the first objective of reflective thinking. Privacy helps ensure that it is unconstrained by practical demands or social and institutional pressures, to the greatest extent possible. However, at the same time, we don't normally want there to be a contradiction between our public and our private selves.

Critical thinking is concerned with the self as both theorist and agent. It is both the last resort when conceptual theorising and practical deliberation are stumped, and the perspective from which conceptual theory and practical deliberation can be integrated with the subjective self. There can be a seamlessness to explanation across theory and practice, a continuity of attitude, methods and goals. This means, in turn, that there can be a coherence and consistency across theoretical and practical thinking. In this way, critical thinking can serve to narrow the gap between theory and practice. The disjunction isn't removed, but it is narrowed significantly, to be bridged in incremental steps, rather than encountered as a single unbridgeable span.

17. Time, productions and performances

At a very abstract level, an event is a change in state. What is distinctive about actions as a type of event is that an action is the outward expression of an inner life.

Most philosophy of action starts from the premise that action implies agency. The converse – that agency implies action – is not necessarily held as widely. However, this implication follows from the continuity of identity that is the condition of agency. A good way of thinking about this is that actions are always woven into a broader stream of events. A course of action cannot take place outside a course of events; it must always be located inside a stream of events. Heidegger characterised this as the state of *Geforwenheit, thrownness*, the condition of being *thrown* into the middle of events, and I think this captures the idea.

This particular way of formulating the idea of action is designed to avoid over-loading the meaning of action. It implies that an action can be an expression of any of the states of mind, not just those concerned with judgement, deliberation and decision-making.

The outcome of practical reasoning is often, though not always, a course of action. Sometimes the reasoning doesn't conclude in a decision; at other times, a decision is made but never put into effect. There may be number of reasons for this. Conversely, not every course of action is the outcome of a process of reasoning. Many actions can be more accurately considered to be reactions to events; defensive or evasive manoeuvres, rather than initiatives. At other times a course of action may be improvised or simply a routine.

For this reason, I think the prevailing model of action in analytic philosophy over-determines the nature of action. This model is built from desires, beliefs and intentions. Agents have intentions, typically grounded in their desires and shaped by their beliefs, and actions are attempts to actualise a future state that, in some way, is a satisfactory response to the intention. It's true that actions are often accompanied by intentions, desires and beliefs, but they are not necessary. We don't need these in order to have actions; things happen, and because they happen, a reaction or response may follow. Similarly, many courses of action are routine and repetitious, arising from the situation, the roles that are being played, and the demands and responsibilities that go with those roles.

It would be truer to say that the formation of an intention and a strategy to actualise it are a special kind of action, what we might call initiatives. Initiatives imply the possibility that enough control can be gained over the flow of events and a sufficient degree of freedom achieved to put together a course of action. When we consider practical thinking as a process of deliberation and decision-making, we are usually concerned with launching, continuing, or terminating an initiative.

There are many different ways of characterising actions. I want to consider four different categorisations. They are, firstly, distinctions due to scale; secondly, the distinction between initiatives, reactions, and routines; and, thirdly, the distinction between a production and a performance. The final categorisation is the distinction between labour, work, action, and theory that Hannah Arendt discussed in her book *The Human Condition*. This last category provides a link between these ideas and the current level of cultural development;

that is; where we are in terms of historical evolution. The objective of this exercise is to capture the multi-faceted nature of action.

The first distinction I want to draw is concerned with scale. Courses of action unfold over various timescales. In his *Philosophical Investigations*, Wittgenstein introduced the idea of a language game as the smallest unit of discourse, and the form-of-life as the larger unit that it belonged to. If we broaden the scope to actions more generally, we could adapt this idea and treat games as the building blocks from which courses of action are built, and forms-of-life the larger structure into which they fit.

These units are still somewhat small scale, though. They are usually routines that are repeated every day, maybe many times a day. They are the quotidian and routine actions that are repeated day-to-day and week-to week. Running alongside these, there are usually larger scale structures in the form of particular projects and, at an even larger scale, we have lifelong structures, such as careers. Finally, at the most global scale, there are the stages of life, the long arcs that unfold in sequence during a lifetime and which are shaped by the decisions that we make, or have made for us, about education, occupation, where we live, family structure and so on. These different levels interact as mutual constraints, so that the framing structure constrains the projects and the routines, and the projects and routines give texture to the framing structure. They are another example of a *Wirkungszusammenhang*.

The second distinction I want to draw is between initiatives, reactions, and routines. Routines are the small-scale courses of action that are frequently repeated. They are situational, often deriving from the role in which someone is cast or the situation in which they find themselves. Quotidian chores also fall into this category. Because courses of action are woven into the stream of events, there is an unavoidable requirement to deal with these events: to react and adjust to the course things are taking.

The routine and the reactive can easily occupy all the time available. Initiatives have to be worked for. When actions are analysed in terms of intentions, desires and beliefs, it is really as initiatives rather than reactions or routines that they are being modelled. An initiative can be at the smaller scale of routine, but typically initiatives imply something larger, a particular project. At a very large scale, an initiative may be carried though at the scale of a career, and unfold across a lifetime.

The categorisation into productions and performances is concerned not with scale or direction but with substitutability. At a very high level, courses of action can be analysed into two kinds. The first kind, which I will call productions, are transformations. The second kind, which I will call performances, are not transformative. Productions are the actualisation of the external world, whereas performances are the actualisation of the internal – self-actualisation.

In a production, there are inputs, a transformative process, and outputs. In such a process something is created: goods and services, capital, tools and equipment, artworks, buildings, infrastructure, concepts and theories, laws, judgements and institutions. With a production, it is the outcome that is important. If the outcome could be achieved by other means, then potentially some other course of action could have been undertaken instead.

In a performance, nothing is produced as such, but rather, a period of time is occupied in a particular way. A theatrical performance is a paradigm of this kind of course of action. There is a stage, some performers and possibly an audience, maybe some props and, usually, a script, though the script may be minimal and the performance largely improvised. The participants come together, the play is performed, the performers and the spectators depart, the script and the props are put away. Everything is left as it was. What has been transformed is the internal state of the participants, as an event has moved from something to be done into something that has been done. Performances aren't substitutable. Whereas different productions may result in the same product, different performances result in different actualisations.

The interaction of productivity and performance can be understood by analysing the creative arts. In all creative arts there is a production phase and a performance phase. This applies as much to the performance arts as to the literary, visual and plastic arts. In all cases, there is the moment of production, during which an artefact is created, and then, usually, multiple performances.

A play, a film or a novel is not an artefact in the sense that a painting or a piece of sculpture is an object. It is really the script for a performance. The text is a store of information. A play, a film or a novel is the collective name for the set of repetitions of the script as performances. This is so even when the performer is the reader of a novel who in reading the novel is effectively giving a performance at which they are at once sole performer and sole spectator.

Generally speaking, courses of action have both a productive and a performative function, but in some it is the productive function that is dominant, while in others it is the performative aspect. These two categories are not for the most part different sets of actions, but different characteristics of almost all courses of action.

The conceptual distinction is important because the value attached to a production is the value of what is produced; it is external to the course of action. It is what is produced that has value, not the action of producing it. This means that productions are substitutable; if there had been a more effective way of achieving the same outcome, that would have been that course of action that would have been taken. This in turn implies that the reasoning involved in production is instrumental reasoning; the task was undertaken in order to achieve an output or reach an outcome, and instrumental reasoning is the reasoning that connects current inputs to future outputs. Finally, the payback from production is always in the future; what is done now is for the sake of something that will happen in the future. Arendt characterised this kind of action as action *in order to*, action undertaken in order to achieve something.

Conversely, the value of a performance is in the performance; there is no output; the value of the performance is internal to its happening, to its actualisation; a period of time has been occupied in a satisfactory manner. The value of a performance is intrinsic to the action. In consequence, performances aren't substitutable. They can't be replaced by something else; if we did something different, we would actualise something else. The kind of reasoning involved is therefore reasoning by identification and classification. The question is: is this course of action of the right category; does it have the right attributes. Arendt characterised this kind of action as action that is done *for the sake of* something.

Finally, productions and performances characterise the passage of time differently. In a production, time becomes the interval that separates the desire from its fulfilment, the objective from its achievement. It instrumentalises time, because time becomes a constraint: *Do we have enough time* or *Are we running out of time.* This leads to the project management way of thinking, in which time, resources and tasks are the three variables that are being managed. On the other hand, a performance can be valued in anticipation, in the moment, and in retrospect. This is possible because performances are undertaken in order that time is occupied in a satisfactory way. A finite life cannot be a production, because a production projects into the future. A finite life, considered as a whole, is a performance, where the ultimate judgement is about the occupation of time.

Arendt's book provided the inspiration for many of my ideas on this topic. Although it is steeped in an understanding of the ancient world, particularly ancient Greece, it is still relevant today, with the relevance of something that no longer exists but where the differences from what does now exist serve to illuminate ideas that wouldn't otherwise be so apparent.

Arendt built on the ancient opposition between the *vita activa*, the life of action, and the *vita contemplativa*, the life of contemplation. Within the active life there are three possibilities: labour, work, and action.

Her argument is that there has been a reversal in the value attached to these ways-of-living since the start of the Scientific Revolution.

The distinction being drawn between the labour and work appears to be somewhat artificial in English, where the terms are roughly synonymous, but Arendt may have been thinking in German terms where the distinction is between *arbeiten*, roughly synonymous with labour, and *herstellen*, which typically refers to production in the sense of fabrication or manufacture.

By labour, Arendt means activities that are focused on necessity, and in particular, sustenance, reproduction and child-rearing; activities which were characterised by impermanence and repetition and would, in traditional agrarian societies, be typically carried out by the women in the private domain. It's not that nothing is produced, but it is not produced for its own sake. The purpose of labour is to bring abundance to biological sustenance. Even reproduction and child-care were considered only in their necessary aspect. Labour is what is done out of necessity, not because the task has value in itself. It is the chores we have to do. This means that labour is defined by the constraints on the labourer, not the nature of the task or the focus of the efforts. It has three features in particular: it is a chore done out of necessity rather than choice; it is toil, it is physically hard; and it is unfulfilling, being limited and repetitive.

Work on the other hand is concerned with bringing stability and durability to human life. Fabrication and manufacture, the making of things by artisans and craftsmen, as well as creative artists such as painters and sculptors, are work. Objects, which have permanence, bring stability and durability, whereas the necessities of life are transient, they are produced and consumed, and the labour must be repeated continually.

Public life is the domain of action: politics, administration, law, war and strategy. It would have been the domain of men in the public sphere. The purpose of action is to bring freedom and solidarity-in-plurality to human affairs. In order to fulfil this purpose, action was primarily a method of self-disclosure. What I think Arendt was referring to when thinking about action was a speaker in a court or parliament or on a platform talking to a public, an audience of their equals, that were evaluating the discourse, not simply as spectators, but as engaged participants in a common project.

These distinctions reflected both the underlying philosophical assumptions and the class structure of agrarian societies, with necessary labour and work carried out by the lower classes and public life reserved for an elite. The apex of this structure was an educated leisured class, free from the burdens of necessity, who could devote their time to theory. The *bios theoretika* was made possible by the toil of others. The life of the mind was characterised as the life of quiet detachment from the distractions of an unquiet world of action, work and labour.

This model was always a reflection of the way of life of a particular place and time, the agrarian economies and city-state polities of antiquity. However, the cultural renaissance of the western world is grounded in that inheritance, and so it occupies a large place in our cultural imagination.

There are, I think, a number of evolutions that this model doesn't take account of. The traditional notion of theorising and the privileged position given to contemplation also reflected the pre-scientific situation. As Arendt noted, the Scientific Revolution was predicated on the invention of the telescope and the microscope, and has continued in a kind of dance with the development of technologies, which are both driven by the requirements of science and provide the instruments necessary to its practice.

The productive capacity of the modern industrial economy is on a vastly different scale from the traditional agrarian economy. As a consequence of specialisation, productive output is the output from a set of co-operative tasks rather than a single creative effort. There are few domains of work where it makes sense to speak of a single creative agent.

Furthermore, the division of labour in the modern economy means that each person's tasks are only a component of the whole. This means that, for any individual, tasks are not undertaken to create an output but to earn a living. There is almost always this duality, the task of earning a living, and the task of carrying out labour, or a project. Chores can turn up in all courses of action because there will always be processes that are necessary to the completion of the whole project. Even in the most creative activities, there is a requirement for rehearsals and repetitions.

This has created the problem of boredom and alienation, of effort disconnected from purpose. Industrialisation, at least in the well-developed stage, has done much to reduce toil, without changing the necessity or the boredom of labour. In fact, specialisation means that the necessary and the boring become the whole of the task, if a task is both necessary and boring.

It is also arguable whether or not objects – that is, fabricated things – are now the primary source of durability and stability. I would argue that in the modern world, durability and stability are more the consequence of institution building than they are the consequence of the construction of the built environment. The productive capacity of the modern industrial society has made artefacts into throw-aways.

Furthermore, there has been an evolution in the nature of the social structure. It was accepted, at least by those who enjoyed a privileged position, that the toil of some was necessary to the cultivation of the elite. The democratic spirit doesn't accept this. The actualisation of the self, the domain of action in Arendt's system, has been democratised.

The concept of action as self-disclosure and solidarity-in-plurality made most sense in the small city-states of the ancient world. We can understand how in modernity this mutuality has become problematic. There is only a certain scale that can be achieved before spectators start to outnumber participants, and rather than plurality and mutuality, we get the asymmetrical relationships that characterise modern mass societies.

18. Personal autonomy

I have argued that subjectivity is built out of point-of-view and agenda and that subjectivity is the pre-requisite for interiority, which I have characterised as subjectivity with self-awareness, which brings with it a capacity for rationality. Interiority, in turn, is the basis of agency and the capacity for action, where action is understood as the outward expression of an inner life.

In these last two sections I want to consider the government of action. The way I have characterised action leaves open the possibility of irrational and ungoverned actions. Government has two possible loci. It can be internal to agency or it can be external, either autonomous or heteronomous with respect to agency. Autonomy and heteronomy can come into conflict, because they posit different and therefore potentially conflicting sources of authority. However, I will argue that they are also both forms of government, and therefore share the characteristics of government, and this creates the possibility of congruence between the two.

Autonomy can be synonymous with agency. However, there are some significant distinctions that this obscures, and there is a value in distinguishing human agency from personal autonomy. The distinction can be grounded in ideas about rationality, independence, personal discretion, psychological unity and accountability.

Most animals' lives are internally co-ordinated; they can be said to have a point-of-view and an agenda. That is what it means to be a sentient animal rather than a plant. However, for the most part, animal lives follow a routine pattern. Stretching the concepts of agency and autonomy to an insect or a gastropod would empty them of meaning.

Among other groups such as cephalopods and mammals such as cetaceans and primates, behavioural patterns are diverse and sophisticated enough, that is, there are sufficient degrees of freedom, that alternative courses of action are genuinely possible, implying that something akin to agency, of self-direction, though not necessarily of a self-aware kind, extends beyond human beings.

However, we can consider agency to be a human capability without prejudging the evaluation of animal capabilities, which it is always possible that we underestimate. I will use the term *human agency* rather than just *agency* to avoid the difficulties of trying to align this model with biological and physiological classifications.

Human agency implies a reflective grasp of the idea of personal identity and self-hood. Because it is reflective, it comes packaged with the use of symbolic and abstract language and the possibilities of communication detached from the here and now. It is this which allows the idea of personal identity to be conceptualised. It is also this detachment which makes possible the distinctively human capacity for misdirection, the capacity to obscure one's true intentions and feelings, even from oneself. This level of agency is something human beings will find very difficult to throw off; doing so would require a labour of self-destruction. This is a level of inescapable self-direction.

We are looking for another mode of human agency. In order for the concept of self-government to mean something, there has to be a gap between the state of self-direction that agency implies and the state of personal autonomy.

The nature of personal autonomy is probably easier to see by observing its absence. The exercise of self-direction comes in many varieties, and I will consider two somewhat extreme variants. On the one hand, there is a mode of agency that is routine, rigid and unresponsive to events and, on the other, a mode which is wayward and impulsive.

The first describes the situation where the possibility of alternative courses of action isn't recognised, resulting in a way of life lived in inward conformity to prevailing routines and an inner dialogue that doesn't move much beyond thinking *How else could things be*. I would distinguish this from social conformity, because social conformity can mean an outward compliance accompanied by an inner reservation. Social conformity can be a strategy. What I have in mind is more the situation where the routines have been internalised and rules adhered to are assumed to be authoritative and never put into question.

The second applies to situations where alternative courses of action are recognised and acted upon but in a wayward and impulsive manner without a plan, strategy or ordering principles, and the course of action initiated doesn't connect the present state of affairs with any imagined future states of affairs. The judgements and decisions of human agents aren't always good judgements and decisions. They don't have to follow from any process of rational deliberation or result in decisions that can be justified and explained to anyone, including the decision-maker. Human agents can be wayward and impulsive, chaotic and unpredictable, exercising an agency unguided or constrained by any ordering principles.

This situation can arise for various reasons. *Akrasia* or weakness of the will is the state where the intention to do something is not accompanied by the ability to carry it through. It is also possible for someone to be in the grip of an obsession or a compulsion to the extent that their actions are no longer under internal control. There is a further possibility, which is that the avoidance of ordering principles springs from a deep-seated character trait, an aversion to the state of being an agent and the consequentiality of actions, which leads to the rejection of rules and principles, even when they are one's own rules and principles and made for oneself.

This raises the question of whether agency is sufficient for accountability. The intuitive answer is that accountability is a feature of agency, because making it a feature of autonomy would mean that accountability for one's action could be sloughed off through negligence and carelessness, which can't be right.

If, like this, we approach the concept of personal autonomy by the negative way, it can be characterised as the recognition of the possibility of alternative courses of action and ways-of-living accompanied by the integration of judgements and decision-making into a reasonable unity. Human agency becomes personal autonomy when discretionary choices are guided and constrained by ordering rules and principles that generate courses of action with a synchronic and diachronic unity which can be explained and justified.

This is not always clearly apparent. Sometimes, not-having-a-plan is the plan, a conscious decision to act in a way that is difficult to read because it is wayward and impulsive. Conversely, apparent rationality can be a façade, a Potemkin structure of rationalisations and pretexts, rather than the actual decision-making process.

These considerations also point to a degree of psychological unity as something that is necessary to the exercise of autonomy. Conflicts and contradictions can't always be resolved, but the tensions can be managed sufficiently to pursue a consistent and coherent course of action.

The advantage of this model is that it recognises the two sides of personal autonomy or self-government: the *self* or personal component; and the autonomy or *government* component. Unlike human agency, which is difficult to escape, personal autonomy can be lost, or never acquired.

Personal autonomy is a form of government and is therefore salient for both ethics and politics. The ethical question connects autonomy to values. One pertinent question is: what ethical constraints and principles will autonomous agents regard as authoritative? A second is whether everyone should ideally seek autonomy, and seek to initiate and shape the course of events, or whether there should be a division of labour in this regard.

This second question then leads into the political question and the relationship between personal autonomy and social order. The intersection of political liberty and personal autonomy is fundamental to questions of political legitimacy. Is a society of autonomous agents desirable, or even possible? Must the expression of an uncompressible autonomy of individuals be contained and frustrated to some extent, maybe even undermined, in order for society to function. Are autonomous agents inevitably in conflict? This is the question of liberty in its multiple dimensions: intrusion, containment, direction, interdependency, imposition, impersonation, misrepresentation, exploitation, deprivation and exclusion.

These political issues are largely concerned with autonomy versus heteronomy, self-government contrasted with government by others, and government-from-the-inside against government-from-the-outside. I will consider the political question in the next section. In this section, I want to consider the link between autonomy and social roles, and between personal discretion and institutional depth.

If personal autonomy is a state, its presence is observable in the exercise of personal discretion. Discretion is the exercise of decision-making capacity. Decisions are not made in isolation, but always in the context of a collection of social institutions. These institutions create a social environment which manifests itself as a set of roles.

Roles are institutional constraints on the exercise of personal discretion. Almost every activity implies the adoption of one or more institutional roles. There are any number of institutional roles and we play different ones at different times: friend, host, guest, spouse, parent, child, neighbour, bystander, employee, employer, contractor, buyer, seller, client, lender, borrower, investor, agent, advisor, teacher, student, patient, expert, public servant, combatant, law enforcer, informant, advocate, witness, complainant, defendant, juror, magistrate, candidate, voter, representative, legislator, counsellor, chairperson, citizen, principal.

In addition, there are the roles that follow from the initiation of projects. Project roles, such as strategist and tactician, have an instrumental dimension. Given a set of tasks to be achieved, and the constraints of time and resources, our forces have to be organised. In this way, adopting a project role brings with it a set of instrumental constraints to add to the constraints defined by social institutions.

Every role comes with rights and duties, privileges and obligations. The variety and reach of these roles and the breadth of possibilities that they support gives a society its institutional depth. As constraints on personal discretion, these therefore have two dimensions: what is the scope of the obligations and permissions that attach to a role (how binding are they on the role); and to what degree is adoption of the role itself discretionary?

The rules that attach to roles can be of three kinds: constitutive, regulatory and rules of adherence. There is a usually a combination of all three in any situation. The constitutive rules define the role. The rules of adherence are the rules that determine who can or must adopt the rule and who cannot or must not. Regulative rules are the requirements and prohibitions that apply to the exercise of the role.

The concrete constraints on personal discretion in a situation will depend therefore on a number of factors: the degree to which there are constitutive rules that define a set of roles, the degree to which the adherence to the role is discretionary or mandated, and the degree to which the regulative rules that govern a role allow room for discretion and interpretation.

The broad development of modern western societies has been a move away from mandating roles: away from the imposition of roles according to classifications such as social class, gender and age, and a movement towards personal discretion. Expectations around occupations, family life and participation in social networks are much more discretionary. This can be characterised as a general distancing from the essentialist conception of roles. This is the real meaning of individualism.

At the same time, there has often been a parallel development towards a more demanding set of responsibilities to go with many roles. So, for example, with regard to family structures, the rules of adherence have tended to become looser and, in parallel, the regulative rules have tended to become more stringent.

Parenthood and family structure is a good example. There are no longer the same assumptions about who can and cannot become a parent – or indeed that everyone will become a parent and take on the responsibilities that go with that role. At the same time, those responsibilities have become more closely defined and limited, for example by the expansion of the rights of the child. There has been a double evolution: the rules of adherence, the expectation of parenthood, have loosened; and, at the same time, the role of the parent, the constitutive and regulative rules, have become more demanding, so that what might in the past have looked like normal parenthood would be considered negligent today.

While people still have families, neighbours, occupations, social and cultural networks and economic and political roles, and the limits on personal discretion that accompany these, there is an increasing assumption that a large measure of personal autonomy will have been exercised in adopting these roles and can, up to the same point, be equally exercised in leaving them. This separation between roles and individuals is the reason modern industrial societies can be characterised by both institutional depth and extensive personal discretion.

Institutional and project roles bring organisation and order. There is therefore potential for congruence between social organisation and personal autonomy as the exercise of personal discretion according to a set of organising and ordering principles. Whether or not this congruity is realised depends on the nature of the organising and ordering principles in each case.

This demonstrates both the extent and limits of personal discretion. Personal autonomy extends to choosing to take on a role and exercising a level of discretion governed by the role, but it rarely extends to defining it. Roles and institutions are usually the outcome of social and cultural evolution and, in most cases, they evolve, like languages, without any central authority. They aren't part of any individual's personal discretion. However, their evolution can be influenced through the political structure, and it is through politics that the potential for conflict between personal autonomy and external government is sharpest.

19. Degrees of freedom

Autonomy and liberty are connected concepts in the sense that the exercise of autonomy requires a corresponding freedom of action. Personal autonomy and personal liberty are both ideas about constraints; personal autonomy is concerned with internal constraints that are self-imposed; personal liberty is concerned with the external constraints that might thwart or hinder the courses of action which are the outcome of the exercise of the discretion which flows from personal autonomy.

External constraints can take many forms; there are structural constraints, natural constraints, cultural constraints, social constraints and political constraints; these represent the set of surrounding environments within which existence finds itself situated.

Each set of constraints has its own level of necessity and carries with it a set of conditions that define the horizon of what is possible. No type of constraint is immovably determined: it is always possible to direct a course of action to change the horizon. However, like the actual horizon, while the horizons that define the possibilities of a course of action can be shifted, they cannot be transcended.

Structural constraints flow from the inwardness of practical rationality and the structure of decision-making. Natural constraints are the constraints that flow from existence as a physical and biological entity. Cultural constraints are a product of the level of technological and cultural acquisition that has been realised by that culture. Social constraints flow from development of social organisation, and political constraints from the development of political organisation.

Structural constraints are the constraints that are built into the exercise of personal autonomy. They are the consequence of the structure of the decision-making process.

Decisions aren't isolated events; they form a structure with both synchronic and diachronic dimensions. There is a multi-layered structure to action. The architecture is governed by the structuring of time, and the layering is a reflection of the scale and the ramifications of decision-making. At the largest scale, there are significant organising decisions: the structural decisions that create the framework for particular projects and daily routines. This large-scale framework evolves slowly and has global ramifications for the small-scale and routine decisions that are continually made and remade. But there is also a reciprocal dependency between the scales. The global framework constrains the routines and repetitions of the small scale, and the routines and repetitions of the small scale constrain the evolution of the large-scale framework.

Between the global and the quotidian there is the set of particular projects. A project is a framework that organises courses of action around objectives and strategies. Strategies are devised to achieve long-term objectives by bringing consistency and coherence to judgements and decision-making. They are designed to communicate direction, co-ordinate efforts, and measure progress. For a project to have a shape, instrumental constraints must be applied to objectives and strategies to give them the structure necessary to survive the inevitable turbulence of events. The strategy includes the set of working principles adopted to guide and constrain actions in order to bring consistency and coherence to complex and often opaque situations. At the same time, strategies can't anticipate every possible scenario. There is a need for tactical flexibility to adjust to unforeseen situations.

Structural constraints flow directly from the nature of practical reasoning. There are two aspects to this. There are the narrower constraints of instrumental rationality. Strategies must be devised that connect the current state to the projected future state. There are also the broader demands of rationality that connect project objectives and strategies to world-views, the global framework of beliefs, intuitions and forms-of-life.

Diachronic structural constraints flow from the sequential ordering of decisions and actions that flows from the exercise of autonomy in time. The course of a life is path-dependent, a trajectory through a garden of forking paths, and taking any one path both closes down some paths and opens up others. Future decisions are constrained by past decisions. This is a reflection of the nature of decision-making: when a decision is taken, a decision-maker has less freedom the moment after the decision is taken than they did the moment before. If the decision is a significant one, that gap may be substantial.

Natural constraints are the constraints that arise from the way the world works. As natural systems and structures are not the outward expression of an interior life, there is no other self that can be challenged, persuaded, appealed to, or made the object of demands. Natural constraints must be worked with rather than railed against and are as much a positive as a negative. In Kant's vivid phrasing, the dove depends on the resistance of the air in order to be able to fly.

Cultural constraints are the consequence of the state of cultural acquisition. From the individual perspective, cultural constraints will appear as ineluctable as natural constraints. In fact, natural constraints are filtered through technological and organisational levels of development. The frontier between what is natural, what is cultural and what is social and political is not fixed. These dynamics interact to create a loosely integrated environment.

Like rules, social and political constraints can be classified into the three kinds: those that are concerned with constitution, those that are concerned with regulation, and those that are concerned with adherence.

Constitutive constraints define social and political institutions. An example would be the roles and responsibilities of public office and the method for distributing such roles. The rules that determine what constitutes property ownership would be another. At the largest scale, nation states and international organisations have constitutions which define their existence and organisation. Institutional decay follows when constitutive rules are neglected.

The constitutive rules that define an institution will specify how regulative rules are to be formulated and applied. Regulatory rules are applied to courses of action and are typically prohibitions; they tend to take the form of prohibitions on fraud, violence, intimidation and exploitation. They are concerned with transactional ethical requirements, questions of negligence, due diligence and so on, and with the principles that determine success and failure.

The rules of adherence define the requirements for adherence to a social or political institution and how far adherence is a matter of personal discretion. There is a gradient running from voluntary adherence to the institutions of civil society through to the more or less mandatory requirements that flow from law and state.

These rules interact dynamically. If adherence to an institution is voluntary and lack of adherence carries no significant cost, then the question whether its constitutive and regulatory rules are overly irksome will become less significant. On the other hand, if adherence is hard to avoid, then the strictness of the constitutive and regulatory rules that it imposes becomes more pressing.

Within the category of social constraints, we need to distinguish between those that are a consequence of belonging to any social institution and those that are a consequence of the particular characteristics of a given institution. It can be difficult to disentangle the constraints that belong to a particular social order from the constraints that will flow from any social order. Even in the most constructive, circumspect and courteous societies we are going to get in each other's way. In particular, the imposition of tasks and burdens and the setting of conditionalities and interdependencies will be inseparable from any social order. Liberty doesn't lie in the absence of society. A solitary person avoids interference from others, but it's not obvious that their scope for action is greater. In most cases the penalty is that much less is possible. Similarly, flourishing in any domain requires a level of accommodation to the way in which social institutions must be structured.

Finally, political liberty is the level of freedom that is enjoyed within a political framework, within the framework of law and the exercise of power. Political institutions are often the source of the most pressing and the most arbitrary constraints.

Political liberty, like any form of liberty, is an idea about agents, outcomes and constraints. As the legal theorist Gerald MacCallum argued in his article *Negative and Positive Freedom*, the concept of liberty posits a triadic relation. In this formulation, statements about liberty always take the form of statements about an agent, an outcome (specified either in terms of a means or an end), and the set of constraints which function to hinder and obstruct the agent from undertaking the means or realising the end.

MacCallum was critiquing the influential analysis of the concept of liberty that was particularly associated with Isaiah Berlin. Berlin identified two kinds of liberty: negative liberty, which is measured by the absence of external constraints on agents; and positive liberty, which is measured by the inability to achieve a desirable outcome.

This dichotomy can lead to some unhappy results when linked to political disputes. Negative liberty is characterised as the absence of interference by others. Reliance on this view would imply that a person who is prevented from doing something by, say, deprivation or exclusion, would be considered to have acted freely, so long as no one else was directly obstructing or hindering them. This of course misses the structural character of so many constraints. This is the general idea of liberty in the classical liberal and libertarian traditions.

Advocates of positive liberty, on the other hand, can find themselves arguing that, because people often make poor decisions which undermine their own interests, they can only be free if someone else makes decisions on their behalf which lead to them achieve the desired state. This approach requires a concrete idea of a desirable end-state – some form of teleology such as Hegel's. This is perhaps why Berlin particularly associated the idea with the British Hegelians T. H. Green and F. H. Bradley.

Instead of a duality of negative and positive liberty, MacCallum's formulation suggests that liberty is a summary term that stands in opposition to a number of different, and therefore potentially conflicting, constraints. A short list might include: containment, deprivation, direction, exploitation, exclusion, interference, dependency, intrusion, imposition, impersonation and misrepresentation. A long list would break these categories down into a more concrete set of specifications.

For example, there are various forms of containment, such as captivity and imprisonment, but also different forms of spatial confinement which don't always require walls, and various forms of direction, of which enslavement is the most extreme. Similarly, there are many forms of interference and intrusion, from assaults on the body to the denial of privacy and personal life.

Freedom of action can be constrained both by exclusion and deprivation and by the imposition of burdens and interdependencies – by having too little and by having too much. I have included impersonation and misrepresentation as categories because they seek to diminish or remove an agent's control of their self-presentation. Where intrusion exposes, impersonation and misrepresentation hijacks, denying influence over the course of events. Finally, by exploitation I mean the ability and willingness to take advantage of inequalities, as a consequence of asymmetries of information, wealth, influence, precarity and so on. Exploitation is not always easy to see, because the idea is that actions that might be acceptable between equals are not acceptable between the unequal.

Political constraints arise from the political conditions, and political liberty is the focus of attention because it is most obviously open to significant change. It's difficult to change structural, natural, cultural and social constraints in the short term or through a project or a course of action. It is this last category that is in question in discussions of liberty because it is these constraints that, because they are the result of political choices, can also be changed by political action. The argument is over the degree to which particular political constraints are just or unjust, and whether, even if they are unjust, they can be changed without inflicting a greater harm.

There are a couple of broad conclusions that can be drawn from this analysis. The first is that freedom is complicated. The exercise of personal autonomy depends on two factors. There is firstly the inward actualisation of personal autonomy in the realisation of self-government, and, secondly, the state of the surrounding natural, cultural, social and political environment, which may press more or less lightly on the possibilities that can be exercised.

The second is that there are structural constraints on the exercise of personal autonomy. Government, whether adopted inwardly or imposed from the outside, has a structure. Personal autonomy, because it is a form of rationality, can be exercised in harmony with natural, structural and social and cultural constraints. The possibility of congruence between personal autonomy and the political order largely depends on how well the constraints that originate in personal autonomy align with the constraints imposed by a particular state.

V. CONCLUSION

20. A reasonable pluralism and the spectacular diversity of things

There are three families of ideas that appear to be viable ontologies today: naturalism, mysticism and idealism. My view is that religious belief can follow from and be expressed in each of these forms and isn't a separate family as such.

These families don't fall into neat distinctions, so that what is at stake has to be teased out. Philosophical naturalism posits that the human mind is continuous with the target objects of the natural sciences and will eventually be brought within their scope. One aspect of the project of naturalism is therefore to explain the mind in scientific terms and to find in the structure of nature the basis of mind.

The implausibility of this position is an argument about the limitations of the scientific method and the causal closure of the natural sciences. There are many things that natural science doesn't explain: design, engineering, construction, craftwork, agriculture, horticulture, forestry, hunting, industry, trade, markets, war, diplomacy, history, the performing arts, the visual arts, the plastic arts, the literary arts, medicine, law, finance, administration, politics, ethics, life, emotion, attitude, logic, language, mathematics, epistemology, ontology and even science itself. Naturalism fails when it comes to understanding concepts.

The hope is that some future science will succeed and, while we wait for the sciences to make sufficient progress, the question should be deferred. I think this hope is bound to be disappointed. This is not because I think there is a mysterious entity called mind or consciousness that is beyond the reach of the scientific method. My view is that all structures and systems are physical systems. My expectation is that a future neuroscience will discover how the mind works as a physical system, and that it will one day be possible to map mental states and processes to neurological states and processes in the same way that, in computer engineering, we can map software algorithms to electronic logic gates. It will be disappointed because such a science will be able to describe but not explain the workings of the mind, in the same way that physics and chemistry can describe but aren't sufficient to explain living organisms.

The irony is that, were the project of naturalism to succeed, it would look very like a form of mysticism. This is how the physicist Freeman Dyson described his own view:

> I am a practicing Christian but not a believing Christian. To me, to worship God means to recognize that mind and intelligence are woven into the fabric of our universe in a way that altogether surpasses our comprehension.

If the project of naturalism were to succeed, it would end up demonstrating that mind and intelligence are indeed woven into the fabric of our universe in the way that does altogether surpass our comprehension.

Idealism and mysticism are rejections of naturalism. Like naturalism, these labels can be applied to many different sets of ideas, but I think they are helpful as a means of marking an important distinction in focus. Mysticism and idealism tend to be confounded, because both the mystic and the idealist see the basic structure of reality as in some way mind, or as having mind woven into it. I suggest that mysticism takes contentless thought and unmediated experience as central, while idealism takes conceptualisation as central. Where the focus is on the mind, the outcome will be a form of mysticism; where the focus is on conceptualisation, the outcome will be a form of idealism.

Mysticism, like naturalism, takes the unobservable to be real, but disagrees on the nature of that reality. In terms of method, mysticism places emphasis on the reliability of personal experience and, because not everyone can have the experiences, the reliability of the testimony of such personal experience. There are, I think, two fundamental problems. The first is epistemological and is what I have called the fallibility of the mind. The second is logical; ideas don't have meaning in themselves; one thing acquires meaning through having a relationship with something not itself.

There are levels of existence where the categories of mind and matter apparent at the scale that we observe no longer apply, but at the same time, the distinction between these also ceases to have an application at these scales. The materialist will call the result matter, while the mystic will call it mind, but these labels have no meaning when the dichotomy that gives it force has been erased. If the endpoint of naturalism lies in alignment with mysticism, then the converse holds, and the endpoint of mysticism will resolve into a form of naturalism.

With regard to idealism, the focus is on conceptualisation rather than mind. There are many forms of idealism, but what they have in common is an idea about the necessary connection between logic and ontology, implying that the meaning of a concept captures the essence or definition of an object and that definition plays a functional role in the evolution of actualised entities and events. Typically, the principle of sufficient reason will occupy in idealism the place that the causal closure of the sciences occupies in naturalism.

The scope of idealism is the set of objects that are determined by their concept. This tradition has a long history, running from Plato and Aristotle, through Leibniz, Hegel and Schopenhauer to contemporary modal ontologies and the continuation of the old metaphysics in Heidegger. I wouldn't include Kant's transcendental idealism in this list, because in Kant's thinking, only phenomenological objects are determined by their concepts and concepts are a product of the mind.

Idealism makes most sense when applied to cultural artefacts and human actions. It makes some sense to say that an artwork or a piece of equipment, for example, has been determined by its concept, since it was conceived before it was actualised. On the other hand, natural objects are the outcome of a complex pattern of working which do not depend of the actualisation of any concept.

Idealism is sometimes taken to imply a denial of what Erwin Schrödinger called the hypothesis of the real world or the belief that there is a real world out there. But I don't think there is any serious proponent of the idea that there isn't a real world out there, even in the case of George Berkeley's immaterial idealism, the idea that reality is an idea in the mind of God. Rather, the problem for idealism is the inverse of the problem of naturalism; namely, that the dynamics of natural systems are only contingently related to our conceptual models.

If naturalism and mysticism can't find a place for ideas in the cosmos, and idealism can't find a place for nature, where do we go for an adequate understanding.

The co-location of interiority and rationality is, in my view, the distinguishing feature of human existence. The two go together, but they do not have the same origin. Subjectivity and consciousness are outcomes of evolution. Conceptual thinking, on the other hand, is not an evolutionary product, and therefore interiority, which is a combination of both, is also not an evolutionary product.

In his book *Mind and Cosmos*, Thomas Nagel writes:

> *The great advances in the physical and biological sciences were made possible by excluding the mind from the physical world. But at some point, it will be necessary to make a new start on a more*

comprehensive understanding that includes the mind...the question is whether we can integrate this perspective with that of the physical sciences as they have developed for a mindless universe.

I am not convinced that a more comprehensive understanding is the answer. My view is that, more than likely, what we are looking for is a set of understandings, each with a limited scope, but fitting together to cover everything. I would call this a reasonable pluralism. My guess would be that it is actually a widely shared perspective, but isn't recognised because it doesn't have a well-articulated theoretical basis. What I have sought to present in this essay is the outline of what such a theoretical basis might look like.

REFERENCE LIST OF SOURCES

Arendt, H. (1958). *The Human Condition.* Chicago: University of Chicago Press.

Carnap, R. (2005). The Elimination of Metaphysics through the Analysis of Language. In H. Adams, & S. Leroy, *Critical Theory since Plato.* Boston: Thomson.

Cohen, S., & Reeve, C. (n.d.). *Aristotle's Metaphysics.* (E. N. Zalta, Editor) Retrieved from The Stanford Encyclopedia of Philosophy (Winter 2021 Edition): https://plato.stanford.edu/archives/win2021/entries/aristotle-metaphysics

Damasio, A. (2018). *The Strange Order of Things.* New York: Pantheon Books.

Davidson, D. (1970). Mental Events. In L. Foster, & J. W. Swanson, *Experience and Theory.* London: Duckworth.

Davies, W. (2022, June 9). Destination Unknown. *London Review of Books,* 44(11). Retrieved from https://www.lrb.co.uk/the-paper/v44/n11/william-davies/destination-unknown>

Dilthey, W. (1979). The Formation of the Historical World in the Human Studies. In H. Rickman, *Dilthey, Selected Writings.* Cambridge: Cambridge University Press.

Dyson, F. (2002, March 28). Science & Religion: No Ends in Sight. *New York Review of Books, 49*(5). Retrieved from New York Review of Books: http://www.nybooks.com/articles/2002/03/28/science-religion-no-ends-in-sight/

Godfrey-Smith, P. (2003). *Theory and Reality.* Chicago: University of Chicago Press.

Godfrey-Smith, P. (2017). *Materialism, Subjectivity, and Evolution.* Retrieved from Peter Godfrey-Smith: https://petergodfreysmith.com/wp-content/uploads/2018/11/Jack-Smart-Lecture-2017-PGS-E7-Dst.pdf

Hawking, S. (1988). *A Brief History of Time.* London: Transworld Publishers Ltd.

Heidegger, M. (1993). Being, Dwelling, Thinking. In D. F. Krell, *Martin Heidegger: Basic Writings.* London: Routledge.

Heidegger, M. (1993). Only a God can Save Us. In *The Heidegger Controversy: A Critical Reader.* Cambridge, Mass: MIT Press.

Heidegger, M. (1993). The Letter on Humanism. In D. Krell, *Martin Heidegger: Basic Writings.* London: Routledge.

Heidegger, M. (1993). The Question Concerning Techmology. In D. Krell, *Martin Heidegger: Basic Writings.* London: Routledge.

Heidegger, M. (1993). What is Metaphysics. In D. Krell, *Martin Heidegger: Basic Writings.* London: Routledge.

Kahneman, D. (2011). *Thinking, Fast and Slow.* 2011: Penguin.

Kripke, S. (1980). *Naming and Necessity.* Oxford: Basil Blackwell.

MacCallum, G. (1976). Negative and Positive Freedom. *The Philosophical Review, 76*(3).

Nagel, T. (2012). *Mind & Cosmos.* Oxford: Oxford University Press.

Penrose, R. (n.d.). *Closer to the Truth: Is Mathematics Invented or Discovered.* Retrieved from Youtube: https://www.youtube.com/watch?v=ujvS2K06dg4

Plantinga, A. (2012, October 21). *Article: Plantinga – Ontological Argument.* Retrieved from Philosophical Investigations: https://peped.org/philosophicalinvestigations/article-plantinga-ontological-argument/

Quine, W. (1951). Two Dogmas of Empiricism. *Philosophical Review, 60.*

Rutherford, A. (2011). *The Cell: the hidden kingdom.* Retrieved from https://www.bbc.co.uk/programmes/b00m5w92/episodes/guide

Schrödinger, E. (1958). *Mind and Matter.* Cambridge: Cambridge University Press.

Sellars, W. (1962). Philosophy and the Scientific Image of Man. In *Frontiers of Science & Philosophy* (pp. 35-78). Pittsburgh: University of Pittsburgh Press.

Simon, H. (1992). What is an "Explanation" of Behavior? *Psychological Science, 3*(3).

Smolin, L. (2006). *The Trouble with Physics.* Houghton Miffin Harcourt.

Steiner, G. (1991). *Heidegger.* Chicago: University of Chicago Press.

Susskind, L. (n.d.). *Udacity: Why does Mathematics Work? - Differential Equations in Action.* Retrieved from Youtube: https://www.youtube.com/watch?v=2bgZmBAnhdg

Wicks, R. (n.d.). *Arthur Schopenhauer.* (E. N. Zalta, Editor) Retrieved from The Stanford Encyclopedia of Philosophy (Fall 2021 Edition): https://plato.stanford.edu/archives/fall2021/entries/schopenhauer

Wittgenstein, L. (1953). *Philosophical Investigations.* Oxford: Basil Blackwell.

ACKNOWLEDGEMENT

I would like to thank Michael Springer for his invaluable help in editing the draft of this essay and making many suggestions for its improvement.

INDEX

Mendel, Gregor 70, 73

Mendeleev, Dmitri 70

Mersenne, Marin 36

metaphysics 7, 10, 16, 30, 32, 43, 50,
53, 67, 76, 81, 89, 91-93, 95, 114,
142, 160, 243

Mill, John Stuart 82, 106

Modal, modality 3, 41, 57, 91, 108-109,
111-112, 152, 187, 243

monism 181

mysticism 89, 107, 240-244

N

Nagel, Thomas 105, 183, 244

Natorp, Paul 81

naturalism 80, 103-107, 240-244

naturalistic decision-making 127-129

Naturwissenschaften 77, 135

neo-Kantian 81, 85, 100, 160

neuroscience 241

Newton, Isaac 38, 51-53, 56

nominalism 12, 26

O

Oakeshott, Michael 122

observer 35, 40, 54, 58, 84-85, 118, 134,
137, 139-140, 200-201

ontological argument 20-22, 37,
59, 111-112

ontology 1-3, 7, 18, 21, 24-25, 33-35, 47,
83, 86, 89, 97, 99, 103-104, 107, 113,
115, 137-138, 142-143, 173, 241, 243

Oresme, Nicole 26-28

Ørsted, Hans Christian 68

Otto, Rudolf 80, 89

P

passive intellect 19

Passmore, John 99

Penrose, Roger 98, 161, 166

performance 211-212, 214-217

phenomenology 81, 85-86, 114, 138

physicalism 103

physics 2-3, 7, 17, 27-30, 32, 35, 39, 43,
46, 49-51, 53, 56-57, 75-76, 82-83,
86, 97-99, 102-106, 111, 119, 140-141,
160-161, 164, 166, 169, 173, 241

Plantinga, Alvin 111-112

Plato 66, 72, 80, 115, 243

pluralism 5, 107, 168, 240, 245

point-of-view 43, 45, 55, 58-59, 87,
106, 140-141, 167, 174, 180, 182-184,
186-187, 190, 192, 194-195, 197, 201,
207, 209, 222

politics 89, 101, 205, 208, 219,
226, 230, 241

Popper, Karl 100

positivism 81, 88-89, 99-100, 102, 106

www.ingramcontent.com/pod-product-compliance
Lightning Source LLC
Chambersburg PA
CBHW051415090426
42737CB00014B/2684